Help Your Kids Harness Their Inner Powers Through Self-Talk!

At any age, positive self-direction begins with Self-Talk—the kind, loving inner support you give yourself. This is the same kind of positive direction you can give your children with the techniques of *Predictive Parenting*. You can also teach your children to use Self-Talk themselves. Dr. Shad Helmstetter shows you how to teach your children Self-Talk, with simple phrases that are strong, memorable, and immediately useful. With these powerful techniques, children of any age can help themselves gain:

- a clear focus on a positive self-image
- better attitudes—on everything from honesty to homework
- control over special problems and situations—such as concentration, self-direction in school, and behavior in difficult circumstances

And for adults who need help improving their own attitudes as parents, *Predictive Parenting* includes some special Self-Talk designed just for parents! *Now* is the time to begin *Predictive Parenting,* and give your children the key to a fulfilling, successful life!

BOOKS BY SHAD HELMSTETTER

What to Say When You Talk to Your Self
The Self-Talk Solution
Predictive Parenting: What to Say When You Talk to Your Kids
Choices

PREDICTIVE PARENTING

What to Say When You Talk to Your Kids

Shad Helmstetter

POCKET BOOKS

New York   London   Toronto   Sydney   Tokyo   Singapore

POCKET BOOKS, a division of Simon & Schuster Inc.
1230 Avenue of the Americas, New York, NY 10020

Copyright © 1989 by Shad Helmstetter
Cover design by Andy Newman

Published by arrangement with William Morrow & Company, Inc.

Helmstetter, Shad.
    Predictive parenting : what to say when you talk to your kids /
Shad Helmstetter.
        p.   cm.
    Reprint. Originally published: New York : Morrow, 1989.
    ISBN 0-671-67970-8 : $8.95
    1. Parenting. 2. Parent and child. 3. Communication in the
family. I. Title.
[HQ755.8.H454   1990]
649′.1—dc20   89-49619
                                                            CIP
First Pocket Books trade paperback printing March 1990

10 9 8 7 6 5 4 3 2 1

POCKET and colophon are registered trademarks of
Simon & Schuster Inc.

Printed in the U.S.A.

This book is dedicated
to the children.

Contents

1. The Gift of a Lifetime 9
2. The Files of the Mind 15
3. The Birth of a Breakthrough 24
4. Predictive Parenting 32
5. What We Say and Do Not Say 42
6. Making the Key Decisions 53
7. The Rule of Personal
   Responsibility 72
8. A Predictive Parenting Look at
   Self-esteem 81
9. A Predictive Parenting Program
   for Building Self-esteem 90
10. What *Not* to Say When You
    Talk to Your Kids...............................103
11. What *Should* You Say? 116
12. The Messages They Need to Hear.....129
13. The View from the Mind of a
    Child...144
14. Getting Your Message Across 151
15. How Long Should It Take?...................161
16. Discipline, Training, and
    Punishment...173
17. Dealing with the Rest of the
    World..180
18. Setting Them Up for Success.............193

CONTENTS

19. The Powerful Programs of
    Self-Talk 197
20. Predictive Parenting in Your
    Home 213
21. Great Moments of Opportunity 228
22. Your Personal Parenting
    Prediction 235

Chapter 1

The Gift of a Lifetime

 News of the birth of my first child reached me late in the night. The overseas circuits weren't working well that night and most of the long-awaited telegram I received had been lost in transmission. The telegram read, "Happy to inform you of the birth of your child [garbled transmission] . . . 6 pounds, 8 ounces, [more garble] . . . mother and baby doing fine." It was a week later before I finally learned whether my child was a boy or a girl.

I was stationed on an island as a foreign-language interpreter in the summer of 1962, and communications home were limited for a young Naval interpreter. The Red Cross personnel did their best, but during the week of waiting I contented myself with giving out *both* pink and blue cigars until I learned I was the proud father of a baby boy.

It would be a full year before I would be able to go home, become a full-fledged father, and finally get to know my son.

During those long months while I was away, I often thought about how much I was missing. But during those endless days and nights I did the only other thing

I could do. I thought about my young son—and I *dreamed*.

Because I wasn't able to see my son or hold him or talk to him and tell him what I thought, I dreamed and imagined and planned. I created pictures of possibilities, a whole *world* of opportunities and wishes for that young boy.

Night after night as I stood alone on a star-covered hillside, looking out over the miles of ocean that separated me from my son, I thought about what I could do that would make a difference in his life.

Many years later, after living through the dreams and despairs that raising a family creates in our lives, I became convinced that there *is* something we can do.

There *is* something that *any* of us can do to help us bridge the gulf between the dreams we have for our children—and the real lives they end up living out.

What can you do to make a *difference* in your child's life? Is it enough to be a "good parent," provide a secure home, help each child get through the process of growing up, and wait for the day when you can breathe a sigh of relief and send each child on his way?

Or is there something else—something *more* that can be done to help our children get closer to the incredible potentials they were born with?

What *could* you do right now, today, and tomorrow, and the next? If there were one gift that you could give to your son or daughter—*each and every day*—what would it be?

What makes the difference between the dreams we have for our children—and the lives they end up leading?

THE NEXT FEW YEARS
OF THEIR LIVES

I will always remember the occasion of my sixth birthday, when some of my friends and a few relatives were at my home for my birthday party. One of the guests was an old man, a distant uncle named Eli.

Eli had become a friend of mine. He had always taken the time to talk and explain things to me and I remember how hard I worked to keep up with the thoughts about life that old Eli was sharing with me. I thought, even then, that Eli was one of the wisest men I had ever known.

Sometime during the party Eli told me he wanted to talk to me. So we went outside to sit under the trees to talk. "Can you snap your fingers?" Eli asked me after we had gotten comfortable on an old wooden bench in the shade of a pine tree. Being six years old, I immediately told Eli, "Of course I can," and raised my hand to snap my third finger against my thumb in a clear, sharp "snap."

"Snap your fingers again," he said, and once again I raised my hand and snapped my fingers.

"That's good," Eli told me. I didn't have any idea what this wise old man was getting at. But when you are six years old and having one of your first big birthday parties, you don't mind it if one of your old friends wants to teach you something new.

But then Eli took my hand and talked to me very clearly and very carefully. I knew that what he was telling me was important, but it was only later that I realized *how* important it was.

"I'd like you to do something for me," Eli said. "Next year, on your seventh birthday, go outside for a few minutes, all by yourself, and snap your fingers just once. Then, on your eighth birthday, do the same thing again.

11

And do it again on your ninth birthday, and on your tenth. Sometime during the day, or during your birthday party, on each of those birthdays, go off someplace by yourself, just like we're sitting here now, and snap your fingers once."

I agreed that I would do what he said. On each birthday, I would take a moment, go someplace off by myself, and snap my fingers once.

"Then, after your tenth birthday," Eli continued, "snap your fingers once on your fifteenth birthday, and once on your twentieth, and your twenty-fifth, and do it again, once every five years, for every fifth birthday you have for the rest of your life."

By then I was more confused, but I still listened. "Let me see you snap your fingers again," Eli told me, so I snapped my fingers again.

"Since the first time I asked you to do that it has only been a few minutes," Eli said. "But did you notice that by now it seems like there is no time at all between those two snaps? As you get older, you'll start to learn that once time has gone by, it will be nothing more than a snap of your fingers, and you'll wonder where all that time has gone."

"Never forget that it's what you do between those snaps of your fingers that counts," he told me. "If I am still here and can come to your birthday next year, we'll talk about it some more."

My old friend could not come to my birthday party the following year. He went quietly to sleep one night and never woke up again.

But the next year, as I had promised, on my birthday I went out and sat on the bench under the pine tree, thought about what Eli had told me, and snapped my fingers once.

I guess it was at that moment that I first figured out what old Eli had been trying to tell me. The time between that *first* snap of my fingers a whole, long year ago and that *second* snap, one year later, were not even *moments* apart!

A year later, on my eighth birthday, I did the same thing again. I did it again on my ninth birthday and my tenth, and then later on my fifteenth birthday and on my twentieth.

My old friend had shown me, in an incredibly understandable way, what some people never figure out: Once time has gone by, it becomes nothing more than an *instant* in its passing.

On my fortieth birthday I remember walking outside with just myself and my thoughts for a few minutes and snapping my fingers once.

It was true. As I snapped my fingers, I realized again, that all of the years, since the time I did that when I was six years old until the time I was forty, had passed as quickly as though I had snapped my fingers in rapid succession, all at once! The time in between was gone—almost as though I had stepped from the child to the man, in a few brief finger snaps of time.

CATCH THE MOMENTS THAT YOU HAVE

What if you were to snap your fingers right now and mark the date on the calendar? And then, one year from today, when your child is one year older than he is today, do it again? And then again, after another year had passed? The time that passes, each day of your parenting lives, will one day seem like no more than a few fast clicks of time—and it will be behind us.

The moments we have to raise and build the best in our children's lives will, in not too many years, have been fleeting moments that went by all too fast. That is not some philosophical concept; that is simply the truth. Our children are with us for a very short time.

The great moments of opportunity for each of us and for our children are irreplaceable moments in their lives and ours. It often seems like it was only yesterday that we saw our children for the first time. In what will seem like only yesterday, the time we have with them will be gone.

THE GIFT

During the next days, months, and years, there *is* something you can do that will help you give your very best to the children in your life. You can give them *the gift of a lifetime.*

In the following pages you will learn *how* and *why* the words you use when you talk to your kids will affect almost everything about them for the rest of their lives—and how you can literally create for them the source from which all of their future successes will flow.

The children in our lives are *potentials waiting to be fulfilled.* They have so much to offer. Let us see what we have to offer them.

Chapter 2

The Files of the Mind

Let's start our journey by taking a walk upstairs, into the mind of a newborn child. If we could look around in that mind, what would we see? Imagine that we walk into the room where your infant's knowledge about himself and his life is stored.

If there were such a room that we could visit, it would be a vast warehouse—its walls completely covered with filing cabinets. Imagine standing in the middle of that great room, its walls covered from floor to ceiling with the drawers of those filing cabinets everywhere you looked.

Then we walk over to one of the walls of filing cabinets and we select one drawer—and we open it. It is empty. We then select another drawer in the wall of filing cabinets and pull it open; it, too, is empty. And then we try another and another.

As we search through this storeroom in the infant's subconscious mind, we find that almost all of the files are empty. Now and then we find a file drawer that has something in it. But even those files have little in them—they hold nothing more than a small message or two that deals with the child's most basic needs.

There is the beginning of a file on warmth, one on comfort, a few nondescript files that are accumulating feelings of love; one on being held and being close and one or two early files on being hungry and being fed. All of the rest of the filing cabinets in that huge warehouse of files are empty.

Now let's look in on that same filing room a few years later. The child has grown up. He or she is an adult now.

Now we walk over to a bank of files in the adult's mind and open a drawer. This time, when we pull the drawer open, it is full of files! We try another file drawer, on another wall and that, too, is full. So we try another file drawer and another. The room of files that once was empty is now full of every possible file imaginable.

What do those files hold? What do we store in the files of our minds? What are the files we have today—that will control, direct, and affect each of us for the rest of our lives?

If we could walk into the control room of an adult person's mind and look into the files, we would find every word that was ever spoken to him—every thought he had stored—and every moment he had experienced.

Once they begin to get filled up, those files in the mind carry every belief, every picture, we have of ourselves and of the world around us.

Those files hold every notion, opinion, and direction we have, how we feel about every detail of every part of our lives, and what that makes us do about it.

They contain every program that operates our lives today, from how we think we look to how we act or behave, what makes us happy or what makes us sad, what our habits are—good and bad—what works for us and what doesn't, an infinite number of beliefs, attitudes, and feelings that affect what we think and what we do in every circumstance of our lives, what we think we are capable of achieving and what we think we are not, the value we place on ourselves as individuals, and thousands of other, incredibly important programmed details *that make us who we are.*

We can't even begin to review all of the files that are stored in this one mental filing room. That one mind holds millions of files. Every one of them in some way describes the individual whose mind stores them. Every one of them is a program that affects or directs every action that individual will ever take.

CHILDREN LIVE THE RESULTS OF THE FILES IN THEIR MINDS

Most of the files in that mind were given to that person by someone else. And of the most important files that are now directing that person's future—*most* of them were created during the first eighteen years of that person's life.

That entire room of filing cabinets that was empty when we first looked at it got filled up somehow. Every one of those files is a program that was given to that individual, or that he gave to himself. And whether each of those programs was true or not, right or wrong, good or bad, there it is, on permanent file in his subconscious mind.

Those are the files that create every belief, attitude, direction, and action in that person's life. Those are the files that are guiding and directing everything about him. Those are the programs that control his life. *And most of them are the wrong files.*

From here on out, the direction your child's life will take will be the direct or indirect result of everything that is stored in his or her files. Even at this moment, the files that are already stored in your child's mind are determining his or her course in life—from the grandest dream to the smallest daily detail.

Although the actual chemical and electrical process in the brain by which this "mental filing process" actually works is extremely complicated, the *results* of that process are easy enough for anyone to understand. In the simplest summary form, these are some of the principal results that filing process creates in your child's life:

1. *Every decision your child will ever make will be passed by every file that is now stored (or will become programmed and stored in the future) in his subconscious mind.*

2. *A child's directions in life are the results of the files that he or she has programmed and stored.*

3. *A child's subconscious mind will be programmed— his files will get filled up—with us or without us, either by our choice or by someone else's whim or design.*

4. *Everything a child believes about himself or herself is the result of the programs that have been stored in his or her subconscious mind.*

Those mental files become the basic directions for the computerlike program that sets your child's course, altitude, speed, and destination. Those programs, along with your child's genetic makeup and his inborn spiritual guidance, will affect and direct every success or failure that your child will ever create.

WHAT GOES INTO THOSE FILES NOW IS UP TO YOU

At least as long as your child is with you, most of what goes into your child's mental files is up to you. What will you put into them? What destination, what *destiny*, will you help create? What tools will you give your child to help make life better or easier along the way? What beliefs will he or she hold?

The files that end up being stored in your child's subconscious mind form a composite picture of who your child is. They will form the basis for what he comes to expect from life, how he will deal with problems and opportunities, how he will love, care, how he will get along with others.

Those same files will determine how he will measure his own self-worth, how much self-confidence he will have, and how he will feel about trust, honesty, faith, and courage.

Specialists in learning have discovered that our files get filled up whether we *do* anything about it or not—whether or not *we* play an active role in what goes into them.

Even now, as adults, if you and I allow "the world" to continue to fill *our* files at its discretion, without our say-so or control, we end up wondering why so many things go wrong, or why things aren't working out as they should. It is only by taking *conscious choice* in our *own* lives that we can give to our own minds the programs and files that we really want.

The result of that choice—to direct more of our own self-programming—is that we are able to live lives that are more fulfilled. We give ourselves a better sense of direction. We improve our self-esteem and our ability to manage ourselves and our lives.

The same is true for our children. But until they have the ability to take charge of their own programming it is the responsibility of us as their parents and teachers to take charge of what gets put into those files. If we *don't* take charge, if we do nothing about it, their files *will* get filled up anyway. But they will be filled by chance and, for the most part, with the wrong information.

That's why, as an example, a young person's peer pressures can be so disturbing to parents. The vast computer storehouse in a young person's mind will get filled with influences from any source available. And it is a natural characteristic of the programming process, that we are *most* attracted to those *new* programs that are most like the *old* programs that we have already stored.

NEW FILES THAT "REINFORCE" THE OLD

That's how our habits are created. The more we are conditioned in one certain way, our subconscious mind will automatically attract and accept new programs that are similar. If, in the case of a young boy or girl, the old files have been filled with negative programs, new programs of precisely the same kind will be attracted and can easily be installed.

If the young person's self-esteem is low for example, if he sees himself as inadequate, he will be more susceptible to "dares" and to doing things that his friends want him to do but that will erode his self-esteem even more. His unconscious programming that told him he was inadequate will attract *more* of the same kinds of programming from others. And so the cycle begins.

In this case, the influence of peer pressure can get out of hand when there is not *enough* of the right kind of programming in the young person's files to being with. We've known that for years as a fact of "human nature." We now know that it is a biological and neurological fact.

The young person may not be aware of what is going on inside him, and he is powerless to do anything about it. He is simply reacting to those programs that are strongest, which he has on file in his subconscious mind.

The conclusion is unmistakable. If we do not take conscious charge—at least in *part*—of the directives that are fed to our children's minds, the world or someone else always *will*.

But that conclusion also offers us what may be the greatest opportunity that we, as parents, will ever have in raising, educating, and nurturing our children.

Our understanding of the results of the "programs of influence" that we give to our children is not new. But we now know more about how that programming process actually works. And the more we know about how it works, the better the chance we have to make a difference in what goes into those mental files in the first place.

CHANGING THE PROGRAMS

It was many years ago that I first recognized the relationship between the programming we received as children and the way we ended up playing out the rest of our lives as a result of that conditioning. A lot of the programming many of us received was the wrong kind. It worked against us.

I searched for years to find ways that we could *reverse* the old programming and replace it with a whole new set of programs—the kind that would work *for* us instead of constantly getting in our way, upsetting our lives, reducing or destroying our successes, affecting our relationships with others, or in general making life a lot more difficult than it really ought to be.

But the more I worked with adults—to help them learn how to exchange their old programming for a new, better kind of *self*-programming—the more I became aware of a growing inner concern. It was clear that our poor programming was the result of people who raised us not understanding that they were literally programming us—*permanently*—and in many cases in precisely the wrong way. They just didn't know.

WHAT ARE WE PUTTING IN THE FILES TODAY?

But while we are busy trying to help each other, as adults, fix our own programming, the *cause* of the problem is still going on. *We're still doing it!* It's still happening. Many of us are still programming *our* children in the same way we were programmed in the first place. We're still filling the filing cabinets in our children's minds with files that are often negative, vague, misdirected, or simply *untrue*.

By discovering how to change our own "Self-Talk," our own self-programming, we have found a practical solution for changing at least a part of our own past programming. But what about prevention?

What are we putting into the filing cabinets of our children's subconscious minds? If we are still programming our children the same way *we* were programmed, and if many of those programs were the wrong programs to begin with, where will it stop?

If we pass the same sorts of misdirecting programs along to our children, what can we expect will happen to them? And what kind of programming will they, in turn, pass along to their children? Exactly the same kind, of course.

Because of how the brain works, *chemically and electrically,* we live out the programs we were given by others, and we pass them along to our children. A child has an incredible mind, just waiting for us to give it the right direction. And it is because of that mind that there is hope—there is more than hope—there is assurance that you can break the cycle and give your child a better chance.

You can, if you choose, present your children with new programs—a kind of parental conditioning that, once put into motion and carefully nurtured by you, will become a self-generating set of positive new directions in your child's life.

With your child's entire future at stake, the possibilities of what that represents are *positively* overwhelming.

Chapter 3

The Birth of a Breakthrough

The mind of a child is a limitless reservoir, waiting to be filled up. It is an eager, open, accepting, believing, mind, anxious to learn and grow.

But the mind of a child is more than that. A child's mind is also the collective result of the workings of an incredibly powerful human computer—the human brain. And the human brain is, as we have learned, the most miraculous physical creation we have ever known.

Through a remarkable combination of chemistry and electricity, the human brain keeps us alive, learns, and gets us to act on whatever we put into it. It is capable of astonishing feats. That single, powerful organ takes what we feed it (through our five senses and through our thoughts) and literally moves us through life.

The brain contains our attitudes and beliefs, directs and controls our feelings and emotions, determines our actions, and for the most part creates our successes and failures in life.

To understand how the mind of a child works, it helps to understand how the brain works. It is in fact, through the research of neuroscientists that we have begun to understand why each of us thinks, acts, and lives as we do.

THE MECHANISM OF A MIRACLE

In the last decade, brain researchers have learned a great deal about how the brain works. What the researchers have learned has made a profound impact on what we have learned about raising children. I will summarize some of what we now know:

1. The human brain is, in some ways, similar to a personal computer—but far more complex, much more powerful, and not as yet completely understood.

2. The human brain/computer is programmed by our *thoughts,* and through everything we receive through our five senses.

3. "Thoughts" are actually electrical impulses that trigger chemical responses in the brain, which in turn direct or influence our emotions, attitudes, health, and behavior.

4. The brain, and that facet of the brain that we call the subconscious mind, electrically and chemically imprints and stores every word, thought, and picture that is fed to it.

5. The subconscious mind will accept and store what it is told whether what it is told is true or not.

6. The subconscious mind will attempt to *act out* the strongest picture of who we believe we are. If we give our subconscious mind the wrong picture of ourselves, it has no choice but to do its best to make us become the person we were programmed to believe we are.

7. We tend to succeed or fail, have or do not have self-confidence, have or do not have self-esteem, acquire or fail to acquire skills, create or do not create successful relationships, and so on, based on the *programming* we receive or give to the subconscious mind.

8. Every word that is said to us, every belief we have, every experience we have, good or bad, is programmed permanently and carried in the subconscious mind.

9. Most of our programming is received unconsciously—whether we think about it or not, whether the programming is positive or negative, true or false, the subconscious mind listens, accepts the programming at face value—as though it were true.

10. Everything we do in life is affected, influenced, or controlled by the programs we carry in our subconscious mind.

The day we are born we come into the world with an open mind—an open computer—which gets filled up with an immense amount of programming.

In my book *What to Say When You Talk to Your Self,* I wrote that during the first eighteen years of life, the average individual is told no or what he *cannot* do approximately 148,000 times. That is a rather conservative estimate. During the first eighteen years of *your* life, how many times were the no's and the *cannots* balanced with programming from parents, teachers, and friends who told you what you *could* do in life?

Children are told, *"You can't do that," "You never listen when I talk to you," "Can't you do anything right?" "Where were you when the brains were passed out?" "You're just no good at that,"* or *"You'll never amount to anything,"* and a thousand other, equally negative programs. And in every case, the child's unconscious mind—his or her eagerly waiting personal computer—is designed to accept at face value, and program permanently, *anything* it is told! What incredibly poor programming a child's mind sometimes receives!

The result of this is that most of what we come to believe about ourselves is not true—but the brain believes it. That's how programming works.

Everything you say to your child, most of what you *don't* say that the child senses, everything you do—or do not do—every moment of every day is a program that you are giving to your child's subconscious electrochemical computer control center.

WE ARE PROGRAMMING OUR CHILDREN'S FUTURES FOR THEM NOW

If you recognize the importance of that fact, you'll also recognize the responsibility that is carried with it. We do not program children only when we actively or consciously direct them or talk to them; we literally program our child's future, consciously or unconsciously, each and every moment of the days and years that they are with us.

The idea that we, as parents or teachers, are the programmers of our children's minds isn't idle speculation—it is scientific fact. Mind/brain researchers are already mapping the chemical and electrical pathways of our programming in the brain. And there is no longer any doubt that what is programmed *into* the brain the mind will do its utmost to act out.

When you were born, you brought with you a complete set of genetic programs that determined many of your personal characteristics. You were born with your appearance—the color of your eyes and hair, your first and future general size and shape, and your genetic patterns in life.

But add to those genetically programmed chemicals of your mind the day-in and day-out programs that you received from others—and eventually your own *self-programming*—and together they add up to who you are today.

Every single one of your biases, your beliefs, your hopes, your fears, your expectations, your goals, and your image of yourself were the result of programs you received *after you were born*! Not one of those did you bring with you. You received every one of them from someone else—or you gave them to yourself.

CHILDREN LEARN TO PROGRAM THEMSELVES FROM THE PROGRAMMING THEY RECEIVE FROM OTHERS

The way we program children is the same way they will, even when they are very young, learn to program themselves. Their own internal Self-Talk will duplicate the programs that our "Parent-Talk" sets up for them.

That is why the proverb "As the twig is bent, so shall it grow" is scientifically correct—psychologically and physiologically. As parents and teachers, we *do* "bend the twig." We literally affect and change the electrical and chemical directions in the guidance structure of the child's subconscious mind.

If we want the child to grow true and tall, we will have to set this program in the right posture. If we fail to give him the *right* direction, he cannot help but struggle, or grow in the *wrong* direction.

The mind of a child is more than a computer, of course. A child's mind is a mind that is full of hopes and ideas and questions and needs. A child is full of the capacity to love—which a computer is not. A child is a warm and precious living human being. And if you are the father or mother, your child is a part of you. Children are made up of more than the nomenclature of scientists—they are more than neurons and neurotransmitters and the chemical receptors of the brain.

But we would ignore an important facet of our children if we overlooked the fact that they are also made up of the chemistry of their minds.

Most of the books that are written about raising children deal with their emotional needs, their personalities, and their individual behavior. Much of what has been written about them is worthwhile, and there are times when we should take all the good advice we can get.

We have learned recently, however, that if we ignore what goes into a child's mental files—and the *sources* that those programs come from—we will have to confront an endless scenario of unnecessary problems and trial-and-error attempts at getting things right—without ever realizing what we are doing wrong.

Nowadays some of us are learning how to change or override our own childhood programming. Now, as grown-ups, we are finally learning to give ourselves a new set of self-directions, through our own new Self-Talk, that will, in time, make up for some of the negative or incorrect programming we received in the past.

There are today thousands of adults who are working at correcting their old negative programs. They are working hard to replace old misconceptions and false beliefs about themselves with positive new programs of self-esteem and self-belief by changing their own Self-Talk now. (We will discuss how children and adults can improve their Self-Talk in a later chapter.)

But how much better it would have been if we had all

gotten a little more of the *right* kind of programming *earlier*—when we were young.

A PREDICTION OF A CHILD'S FUTURE

Some of what we were told about ourselves was not true about us *at the time we first heard it.* But if we heard it often enough, some of it stuck. Some of us really *believe* that we are not creative or that we will be overweight, that we aren't smart enough, that he or she was not right for us, or that we would never be able to earn the kind of income we wanted to make.

When we were told those "truths" about us, little did the people who were telling us know that they were literally *predicting* our futures for us. And little did they know the power that those predictions would play in our lives.

That is what we, as parents, do. We *predict.* We create a future program that, through a complex process of chemical and electrical activity in the brain of a child, imprints a direction that future events will most assuredly follow.

We direct—and the mind accepts. In a moment of anger we tell a child that he *is* exactly the opposite of how we would actually like him to be:

"You don't even try," "Your room is always a mess," "You think money grows on trees," "You never take any responsibility for yourself," "You're lazy," "You don't know where home is anymore," "You always hang around with the wrong kind of friends."

And somewhere, deep in the recesses of his subconscious mind, the child *stores* that seemingly harmless, unintended, but completely inaccurate description of his potential self. Given enough reinforcement of that new self-belief, the child will eventually act out the harmful direction and make it *true*.

You and I are living our lives today as a result of the programs we received. Some of them were good. Some of them were not. We live with self-perpetuated programs that tell us *incorrectly* that we can't lose weight and keep it off, that we can't earn enough income, that we can't get organized or get to work on time or go back to school or make a marriage work.

Why do we program ourselves with the wrong programs? It is habit. We learned to do it.

Think what you could do with your life if you could rid yourself of every self-defeating program that your own subconscious mind has stored and is helping you act out.

What an exciting legacy you could give to the children in your life if you gave them a completely *different* set of programs. Would it have an effect on their lives? Yes, it would! Imagine playing a major role in creating and predicting a positive, fulfilling life for the child or the young people in your life.

When we give young people the kind of positive programs of *clear, strong, healthy self-direction* that we would like to have had more of ourselves, we give them a gift that will help them for the rest of their lives.

The recent scientific discoveries in the workings of the human brain—and in that facet of our brain we call the subconscious mind—have given us an important new breakthrough in our understanding of how to train and prepare our children better.

That breakthrough is: *Predictive Parenting*.

Chapter 4

Predictive Parenting

The concept of Predictive Parenting is not difficult to understand. And fortunately, once understood, it is a concept that any of us can put into practice. Here's how it works:

The word *predictive* means to predict or to set up a *future condition*. When you parent, that's what you do; everything you will ever do as a parent consciously or unconsciously *predicts*, in some way, a future circumstance in your child's self or life. By your own words and actions you are, whether you're aware of it or not, setting up a *future condition* for your child.

Everything you do or say (or do *not* do or do *not* say) to your son or daughter, intentionally or not, is creating a subconscious program in his or her mind. Because the subconscious mind accepts anything it perceives, right or wrong, you are, in everything you say or do, filling up those filing cabinets in your child's subconscious control center.

TWO DIFFERENT KINDS OF PREDICTIONS

In its simplest form there are two kinds of parenting (or teaching)—both of which influence the future of the child.

One kind is *unconscious*. It can be positive, negative, or neutral in its result, but it is usually *invisible*. We are setting up attitudes and beliefs in our children by all of our words and actions. As a result, we are *always,* in everything we do, influencing and predicting their beliefs and their potential behavior.

This unconscious kind of parenting leaves many of the *results* of parenting up to chance. And it is this kind of parenting that causes us to feel that we lack control; as though there is something else we should do that will make a difference, but we are not sure what it is.

The other form of parenting is *conscious* and it is worked at openly, with awareness and purpose. It is this form of parenting that we call Predictive Parenting.

All parenting, of every kind, *predicts* or sets up the future of the child. But Predictive Parenting is a way of recognizing this, *taking action,* and consciously doing everything possible to set up the best, most positive conditioning for the child or young person.

A Predictive Parent is someone who exercises conscious judgment in every parenting situation and who recognizes the effects of natural programming on each child's future.

Predictive Parenting creates more positive results in a child's life because the parents are more aware of what they are doing, how they look at problems and opportunities, and what the probable results will be down the road. They are aware, every day, of the powerful programs and influences that they are creating in their children's minds.

The result of this is that when you are aware of your role as a Predictive Parent, you consciously give your child more positive directions, create more self-esteem, more self-confidence, and an understanding of personal responsibility. *And you create these important files in precisely the same natural and healthy way we were designed to be taught and nurtured in the first place.*

As a Predictive Parent you also reduce the effects of a child's programming that in the past may have been left up to chance. You look for opportunities to build your child's self-image and create strong, lasting programs that will help develop attitudes and habits that lead to self-sufficiency and success. You literally assume the responsibility for playing a more significant role in the programming that will most positively affect your child's upbringing and future.

PREDICTIVE PARENTING IMPROVES THE PROGRAMS

We now know that the subconscious mind accepts information it is given at face value. When we deliver a message to the subconscious mind, that message is received and programmed in the brain without regard for its truth or accuracy. Because of this, we often end up creating a permanent program in a child's mind without ever being aware of what we've done, or without ever knowing that the program can have far-reaching and possibly negative consequences in the child's life.

Saying something as simple and seemingly innocent to a child as *"Your reading is terrible"* or *"You're just no good at math,"* as an example, can literally create a new program that sets up future failure for your child in that skill and eventually a host of other things that rely on the same skill.

If that simple, inadvertent program sticks, or if it is strong enough to begin with, it will attract *other* programs that support it and reinforce it. In programming the subconscious mind, "like attracts like"; one strong program will attract other messages of the same kind.

A strongly programmed belief in a child's mind that he is clumsy, for example, will cause the child to accept other, additional programs that *convince* him that the first program is *true!* With enough supportive programming, something that was *not* true to begin with becomes true in fact.

I have heard parents (and teachers!) talk about a child's poor reading skills *in front of the child,* as though he weren't even there. And in so doing, they literally created a program for that child's mind that will, in all likelihood, keep him from *ever* becoming an adequate reader!

Eventually, enough negative—but similar—programs get together, and a powerful new program emerges: *Johnny can't read!* He knows it. His parents know it. His teachers know it, all because his subconscious mind was given a program that made it true—even though Johnny once had everything he needed to become a perfectly capable reader. He was born with the potential; he *had* the capability. But the new programming took it away from him.

A few remarks, on the part of the parent or the teacher, said the wrong way at the wrong time, that started the first program of self-doubt about his reading ability in Johnny's mind, literally *predicted* a future circumstance and made it come true.

That same story—the same unfortunate programming—is repeated in all too many ways in so many young lives. It doesn't have to be a few thoughtless words a child hears about his inability to read or spell. It could be anything.

In Johnny's case, the words create a degree of doubt and inability in Johnny's mind that will end up affecting him through a significant portion of his life. That is unconscious, negative, predictive parenting. We do it without knowing it. And without knowing it we seldom recognize its consequences.

That may not be the *only* reason Johnny can't read. There may be other contributing factors. But does your own belief about whether you are capable or not affect your ability? You bet it does! *Your own beliefs about yourself are the strongest programs you carry in the files in your subconscious mind.*

Self-belief is one of the single strongest components in developing skill at *anything*. Assuming he had the rest of the necessary learning capability, Johnny's eventual ability to be a good reader is dramatically affected by the perceptions he got and now holds of himself.

That's true of most of the skills and attitudes that children develop about school, as an example. *Success in school doesn't come from high I.Q. Success in school comes from high I can!*

The results of a young person's self-perceptions affect a great deal more than skills and attitudes in school. A youngster's self-perceptions affect everything about him or her. A girl who is told, even at a very young age, that she is chubby and should eat less or watch her weight, may not think this new parental program is true the first time she hears it.

In fact, when a child first hears some negative statement about herself, it is often far from the fact. She may even be surprised! But give her time, and enough negative conditioning or reinforcement, and she will believe it. Soon her subconscious mind will begin to look for—and find—confirming evidence that what her parents are telling her is true.

The first sign of snugness in a pair of shorts or a dress will send another message to her subconscious mind:

"Your parents were right. You're already chubby and you're going to be fat." Then food will begin to change in importance and value—anything that tastes good will appear to add weight, and each bite will add to an uncomfortable feeling inside called *guilt*. Once-innocent remarks from friends at school will now take on a whole new meaning and importance. In time she will begin to see herself differently every time she looks at herself in a mirror, puts her dress on in the morning, or walks into a room where other people are watching.

For what may become most of her life, that young lady could carry her overweight *programs* with her. Each look in the mirror will reconfirm them, each self-doubt will add new programs to old. And in time, her mother will have been right. The daughter was going to be overweight, and the mother had predicted it.

CREATING A NEW AWARENESS

Predictive Parents do not blame all problems at school, all problems with weight, problems with friends, problems with bad behavior, or all of the other problems children and adults end up with, solely on poor programming. But Predictive Parents are always aware of the role that programming *does* play in every belief that a child has.

Look at anything you feel or do that creates a problem in your life. You will find that your own subconscious programs are *always,* at least in part, responsible for the problem being there in the first place!

This does not mean that every word you utter is going to make a drastic change in your child's future. The subconscious mind is more complex than that. It does not change its programs quite so easily. Usually, something said once or twice, or perhaps even a dozen times, if it is not of great importance, will not automatically set up a new program in your child's mind.

Most of our programming is created through constant repetition of like-sounding messages. Unless a single message is unusually strong and memorable (*"No matter what you do, I will never trust you again!"*), it takes many of them added together to make a difference.

But eventually those programs begin to collect and solidify. In time they begin to create or set up a "pattern or programs," which begin to shape the mind—and the future—of the child.

THE SHAPING OF YOUR CHILD'S MIND

Our children receive a *constant* stream of subtle programs. Even the small, innocent-sounding programs add up.

In time those tens of thousands of quiet, mostly unnoticed comments and actions from parent to child, tell him an incredible amount about himself. Right, wrong, uplifting, or defeating, the mass of minor programs join together and begin to take form. Finally we see a shape emerging. A hundred or so forgotten comments about our child's attentiveness in school finally cement into place his image of himself as a listener, his ability to concentrate, and his mental acuity.

Another hundred words or criticism or praise about such things as his neatness, his promptness, and his ability to finish a job mold into place the shape of the organizational skills that he will carry with him into his future. Several hundred or thousand more words and comments about his manners, his behavior, and his consideration for others weld together and begin to form the face of his personality.

Dozens of passing conversations at the dinner table or riding in the car or sitting by the campfire eventually merge together like steel cables and girders, forming the superstructure of the values that will carry him through his life. Ten thousand other thoughts, most of them never spoken but transmitted through nods and expressions, some in approval, some in condemnation, now weave an intricate fabric of self-image that covers the structure of programs that course through his mind. The shape that these words and thoughts—your programs—create *is the shape of the life of your child.*

In less than a minute's time you can as easily say something to your child that is mentally healthy and nurturing or something that is not. What you say in that one minute will not by itself, in most instances, have a serious impact on your child's programming. But gather together a few dozen of those minutes, or a hundred of them.

If you were to spend only thirty minutes a day for a year within speaking range of your child, that amounts to roughly eleven thousand minutes. That is 182 hours of direct parenting influence on your child's mind in just one year! Over the course of fifteen years that would amount to between 2,000 and 3,000 *hours* of parenting time that you spend with your child.

Whether you realize that you are predictively programming your child during those two or three thousand hours or not, your child's personal computer is listening. It is the combination of those hours of programming that ends up becoming permanent programs in the young person's mind.

SOMETHING YOU CAN DO TODAY

Many parents recognize that their actions and words do condition their children, but they are somehow able to put off actually doing anything about it until "tomorrow" or some other, "more convenient" time. While a child is growing up, it seems as though there will always be another time, another chance, another opportunity to spend more meaningful time together, time to get better acquainted or go to lunch together or just talk to each other.

You may, in the future, decide to catch up on some of the Predictive Parenting you wish you had taken care of in the past—but when it comes to parenting, there is never a better time than the present. The right time is right now, every day you are with your child, and even when you are not.

The more we understand how Predictive Parenting works, the more we consciously do and say those things that help us create the future for our children we would most like to predict. If in the past you have felt powerless to be heard, to make a difference, to ensure your child of at least the chance of having a happy and successful life, Predictive Parenting gives you that opportunity. Once you recognize it, it is yours.

A VALUABLE RESPONSIBILITY

Along with the opportunity, you are also given the *responsibility*. In the past, if you were not aware of how strong a role those hidden programs and messages played in your child's development, you did not really have to take full responsibility for them. If you decide to practice Predictive Parenting for a time and then lose interest and put Predictive Parenting off for some other time, you are responsible for the results you will create. But if you accept the opportunity to give your child the benefit of parenting with this new awareness, you can also take responsibility for your *success*—and take pride in your accomplishment!

Most of us who are parents would like to have that sense of inner fulfillment—*knowing* that we did something that *worked,* and knowing that there is something that should continue to work in the future. It's a rewarding feeling.

Nothing can take the place of the exhilaration we feel when a son or daughter looks back at us and smiles. We see our own positive programs—that we gave them—coming back to us. We see a look that says, "Thanks, Mom. Thanks, Dad . . . . It's working!"

Chapter 5

What We Say and Do Not Say

Let's look at a few examples of things some parents say to their children. Some of them are said consciously. Others go by almost without notice. Both have their effect. See if you find any of these that are similar to anything you might say as a parent, or if you know of someone else who might say any of them.

Recognize that the child's subconscious mind electrically and chemically imprints and stores each of these messages as a program that is potentially true or *already* true of himself or herself. And then, think for a moment of what the future *results* of these messages might be.

These are things that children, in their most believing, accepting minds, have been told:

You never listen when I talk to you.
Can't you do anything right?
Close the door. Were you born in a barn?
You're so clumsy.
You're just like your father (or mother, etc.)!
When will you ever learn?
Children should be seen and not heard.

Can't you be more responsible?
You're lazy.
You're impossible!
You're just not cut out for that.
You can try it but I don't think it's going to work.
You'll be the death of me yet!
I don't know why I put up with you.
Just this once, try to tell the truth.
You're always in a bad mood.
You always interrupt.
You always talk when you should be listening.
Haven't I taught you anything?
I'm at my wits end with you.
Why should I listen to you?
Why should I believe you?
Why should I trust you?
Why should I give you another chance?
You're just no good at that!
Your brother (or sister) never talks like that!
What did I ever do to deserve this?
I don't want to hear another word out of you.
All you ever do is complain.
Nothing is good enough for you!
This time try to get it right for a change!
Who do you think you are?!
Your room is always a mess.
You have no respect for anything!
You're always getting into something!
You just don't think!
This is the last time I'm going to tell you.
I can talk to you until I'm blue in the face and it doesn't do any good!
Where were you when the brains were passed out?
Nothing I say makes any difference to you. It just goes in one ear and out the other!

You don't know where home is anymore!
You think money grows on trees!
Don't you know anything?
Sometimes I just don't know about you.
How stupid can you get?
Can't you do anything right?
I just can't talk to you anymore.
Don't you care about anything?
You just don't try!
You think home is just a place to sleep!
I'm through listening to you!
What makes you think you're so special?
I'll tell you what's wrong with you . . .
You think you're so smart.
Can't you get it through your thick head . . .
You don't know the meaning of the word respect.
You're lucky to even be living here!
All you know how to do is cause problems!
One day you'll be sorry.
Just wait till you have kids of your own!
All you want to do is sleep!
All you want to do is avoid responsibility!
All you ever do is talk back.
All you ever do is argue!
Where did I go wrong?
Someday you'll learn!
If you only knew what you put me through.
Talking to you is like talking to a brick wall!
I've had it with you!
You're never home on time.
You never come when I call!
You never care about anyone but yourself!
You never do anything that I don't ask you
  to do.
You never pick up after yourself.
You never finish anything!
You never tell me the truth!

You'll never get anywhere.
You'll never amount to anything!

These statements are a powerful form of the wrong kind of predictive parenting! They predict the *wrong* things, of course, but they, too, set up life-scripts and predict important self-images that the child will eventually accept as true.

Those are examples of negative parenting because they are messages that predict negative results. They are the kinds of things we can find ourselves saying, entirely unaware that we are saying them. And the child, who may be used to hearing such things, appears to ignore them. But the child's subconscious mind *never* ignores them.

The child's subconscious mind listens to each message, carefully evaluates where it should be filed, and looks for other similar files, other beliefs that this new piece of information will support. It hears it, recognizes it, and accepts it. And then the child's mind throws an electro-chemical switch in his brain that records and programs the message permanently and prepares to act it out.

The child's subconscious says, *"I've got the program. Now I'll go to work to make it happen!"*

It makes no difference if the mother or father knows the importance of what she or he is saying. It makes little difference if the child really notices the remark or not, or consciously believes it. The result will be the same. Another program, another *prediction* of that child's self-identity has just been permanently recorded and sealed into place.

Of course, a lot of our Predictive Parenting, even when it has been unconscious on our part, is completely the opposite of the examples we have just seen. A lot of our parenting is excellent and it does our children a world of good. Many of the things we do and say are helpful and supportive, and they predict or set up mental programs that are healthy and supportive. The problem is that as a child grows up, simply because of our society and the world we live in, he receives many more *negative* programs than positive.

Those programs come not only from the parents but from brothers and sisters, friends and classmates, and even, at times, teachers at school. And those are only the program sources that are the most obvious. Tens of thousands of *additional* childhood messages come from television, movies, popular music, and from such seemingly innocent sources as the evening news. Programs come to kids from every side.

Some of them are helpful programs—but *many* of them are not. And the programs that will win out are those that are repeated most often or are the *strongest*.

SOMETHING *NOT* SAID CREATES JUST AS STRONG A PROGRAM AS SOMETHING SAID

It is not only what is *said* to us that gives messages to our subconscious minds. Often just as powerful are those programs that are created by something that is *not* said. Imagine the result of *not* hearing words like these:

That was really great!
You were wonderful!
You really do that well.
As always, you look good today.
You're a winner!
I trust you.
I can always count on you.
You're really smart.

People really like you.
I like the way you did that.
You're really fun to be with.
You make me feel good.
You really take responsibility for yourself.
I like the way you keep your room neat.
You sure have a lot of energy.
You're really positive!
You always seem to be able to keep yourself busy.
*You ended up with the best of both your father
    and myself.*
I really rely on you.
That was close. Next time I know you'll make it.
Good job!
You're beautiful.
You're very pretty.
You're handsome.
You make every day brighter.
You sure have a nice smile.
I listen to what you have to say.
You're a good friend.
You really get along well with other kids.
You're an achiever.
I can tell you're going to be successful in life.
You're very creative.
I've noticed you're a very good listener.
It's obvious that you care about yourself.
You're a good runner.
I'm proud of your schoolwork.
That's much better. You're doing great!
You're really special.
I love you but I like you too!
You make hard things seem easy.
You really practice good manners.
There is no one else like you in the whole world.
I need your advice.
You sure are talented!

Good answer!
Thank you.
You deserve it.
Can I help?

With a little practice it is just as easy to say those things as to *not* say them. And it is worth the practice. That, too, is Predictive Parenting. Saying something that could or should be said creates and stores strong beliefs in the child's subconscious mind. Imagine what programming you would be creating if you *did* say them—not just occasionally, but every chance you had.

Think for a moment of never putting off an opportunity to send a message to your child's future, by helping create an incredibly rich self-description in that child's mind today. Are they empty compliments? They are just the opposite. They are the fabric from which the child's identity is formed.

WHAT MESSAGE WOULD YOU WRITE?

Imagine that for one week you could not talk out loud to your child. Instead, in order to communicate with him you had to walk up to your child and actually type your words into a personal-computer keyboard that he carried in front of him. Also imagine that that keyboard is plugged directly into your child's subconscious mind. And on the keyboard is a sign that reads, WARNING! EVERYTHING YOU TYPE INTO THIS COMPUTER KEYBOARD WILL BE STORED—PERMANENTLY—AND ACTED UPON!

Now instead of *saying* something to your child you would type the message directly into his or her subconscious mind. What do you suppose you would type? What messages do you suppose you would enter into the computer if you knew that those messages—those programs—*would be stored for life and acted out*? Would you "say" the same things to your child's computer that you would say to your child himself?

There is no difference, of course. *That is what all of us have been doing all along.*

We have been typing our words of programming into those incredibly powerful little mental computers, and our kids have been accepting our programs just as surely as if we had walked up to them, sat down at a keyboard, and started to type.

THINGS WE DO OR DO NOT DO

There are other things we say—but not with words. These are the things we communicate to our children by what we do, or do not do. And those actions, too, create strong predictive programs. Examples of ways we create negative programs by things we do—or do *not* do—are:

Always looking too busy
Not showing up for an important event
Irresponsible use of physical force
Losing control or throwing things
Frowning as a response
Leaving the table because of an argument
Storming out of the room
Driving recklessly or immaturely because of anger
Making promises and then breaking them
Putting things off
Not taking the time to talk one-on-one

Not doing things together or as a group
Lying
Doing things you would not want your children to do

I am not suggesting what is right or what is not right for you. I am not suggesting what is appropriate behavior for you and your family and what is not. But I *am* suggesting that you recognize that what you choose to do, how you act, *will* have an effect on the permanent programs and on the permanent identity and beliefs your child is creating every minute of every day.

Children receive a powerful program when, for example, they are taught that it is okay for parents to tell an untruth but that when the child tells a lie he gets punished. A child can be told to tell the truth, but if the parent then misuses the truth himself, the child will become programmed to believe that it must be okay to tell a lie.

Sometime later that child will look the parent straight in the eye and deliver a whopping story that would do credit to Mark Twain! The real credit for the untruth, however, goes not only to the child but to the person who gave the child the program that *created* the lie in the first place.

THE EXCITING RESULT OF BEING AWARE

Even a look or a gesture can imply any number of things to an open young mind. That mind, in one of its most frequent states, is *looking for praise and fearing criticism*. It is your choice, and responsibility, to decide which it will receive.

Each of those eleven thousand minutes of contact that you may have with your child in just one year is a moment of opportunity. In the future most of those moments will probably pass in much the same way as they have in the past. But it is what we do with some of them that will count.

It is not the occasional long discussions we have with our children that program them most, it's the little things we say that add up to be the biggest programs in their minds.

To be a more active, conscious, positive, Predictive Parent does not mean that you have to hover over your child like a guardian angel, praising every move he or she makes. It is far more important to recognize what you can accomplish just by being *aware* of what your words and actions are creating in your child's mind.

It is clear that none of us, in the past, *tried* to predict the wrong kind of identity or future for our children. Much of what we have said to our children and the ways we behaved toward them have been the positive kind of parenting. Most of what we said or did that wasn't, we said or did because we didn't fully understand the effects that we were creating.

It has been only recently that neuroscientists and behavioral researchers have begun to have sufficient understanding of the care and feeding of a child's mind, both psychologically *and* physiologically, that we really know what to do about it. I doubt that I have ever met a parent who said to his or her spouse-to-be, "Let's get married, have children, and program them in the wrong way."

Can you help give your child "success"? Yes, you can. Will everything you do and say, tomorrow and everyday hereafter, make a difference in your child's life? Yes, it will.

Your child will continue to be influenced, conditioned, and programmed whether you as a parent do anything about it or not. Your child's mental control center will stay turned "on" and open every breath of his life.

Knowing that gives us a chance to give our children an exceptional armament of the very best beliefs, attitudes, and actions. And doing it will depend on the decisions we make.

Chapter 6

Making the Key Decisions

To help us reach the goal of being successful parents, there are a few decisions we have to make.

If we want to focus our energies on becoming the best Predictive Parents that we can be, we first have to think about:

Whether we really want to be the best parent possible
What our objectives are
Who will set the direction of our household
How we view our roles as "preparers" or "maintainers" of our children
What our expectations for each child are
Whether or not we will be consistent in our style
What effect our *own* programming, which we got when we were being raised, will have on our own parenting styles and methods

It is when we consciously evaluate each of these parenting decisions that we recognize the role they play in our own parenting. We determine for ourselves what we expect of ourselves, what we personally agree to do, and what we accept or do not accept from ourselves in our roles as parents.

Each of the following "Decisions of Predictive Parenting" gives you an opportunity to decide for yourself where you stand.

They are not "rules" of parenting; they are examples of some of the most important questions about your own parenting beliefs and attitudes that you could ever make. And these key decisions will help you make one additional important decision—a decision that will guide and direct you in everything you say to your children for the rest of their lives.

1. Forgive (Accept) Your Own Parents

Eventually, if you want to be the best parent you can, completely free from past angers and shackles, you will have to accept your own parents and any mistakes they may have made with you along the way.

Have you ever imagined how much of what you feel about your own upbringing affects how you raise your children? For all of us, the influence of our own childhood conditioning is a powerful influence in our adult lives. It is an equally powerful influence in how we, in turn, raise our children.

That is natural of course. That is our programming. What we learned about growing up, from the parents who taught us, is, for most of us, the single strongest set of programs we received during the most important years of our young lives. As we have learned, that's how the mind works—that's how the computer in our brain is programmed.

But what if our parents did not know that everything they said or did would somehow program our personal mental computers to record and comply? What if our parents (who were programmed themselves) did not know that what they put into our mental computers would affect everything else about us from that time forward?

Were our parents to blame for giving us something less than the best of programs? Of course not! *They didn't know!* They did the best they could with what they knew. They responded to their own conditioning in the best way they knew how.

We don't always see the human mind as being that simple, of course. The mechanism of the mind is complex, and it often seems the way people behave is anything but rational. We may not even recognize the tie between what someone else does and the past conditioning he or she received.

But the fact is that sometimes we got less than the best programming from our parents or from the people who raised us. They may have loved us and wanted the best for us, but they raised us based on the programming they received. It wasn't always right. It may have even set us up for some problems in the future. But it was what they "knew."

Unfortunately, the problem of our own past programming doesn't automatically go away at the age of twenty-one or when we begin to raise children of our own. The hidden messages of long-forgotten childhood programs stay with us. And even as mature, thinking, sensible adults we act them out.

Thirty years after our parents may have unknowingly told us to eat everything on our plate, we tell our own child to clean his plate.

It doesn't make any difference if we are struggling with an expanding waistline and twenty pounds of extra weight ourselves, we *still* tell our children to finish all of their food. Why? Because we were programmed to believe we should clean our plate!

But our past programming goes deeper than that. It reaches into the deepest recesses of our unconscious and makes its way into every facet of how we think and live today.

In the vast storehouse of past programs that you keep on file in your subconscious mind, you have dozens of files of attitudes, opinions, and beliefs about your parents, teachers, and about anyone else who might have helped raise you.

How do you feel about them? What thoughts, beliefs, and impressions about them—and how they raised you—do you still carry with you?

It is not difficult to recognize that every piece of information that you hold in those files can, and does, affect a great deal of how you think, what you do, and how you live out each day of your life today. That is a part of what past programming does; it affects everything about us, whether we are aware of it or not.

But unless we put some of that programming to rest, recognize where it came from, decide not to use it, and decide to let it go, it can affect and direct us for the rest of our lives.

Those who raised us did so based on the conditioning and the programming they received. They may have been the greatest leaders in our lives or we may wish that we could have had better. But *all that is in the past.*

MAKE THE *BEST* OF WHAT YOU HAVE NOW

If we got good directions from our parents or from the other people in our pasts, we should be thankful for it. If we did not, we should be thankful that we have learned enough to go on in spite of it. It doesn't take a lot of convincing for any of us to realize that what is past is past; it is up to each of us to make the best of what we have now.

When you realize that your own parents did everything they did because they, too, were programmed, conditioned to think, act, feel, and parent in the only way they knew how, it makes sense to do your best to accept them in the most loving and understanding way. One day your own child, as an adult, may do the same for you.

That's important. Because unless you let go of the unfulfilled wants and wishes you had as a child, you may, unconsciously, try to re-create them in your own children.

If you live a life of leftovers from your own childhood, you could make the terrible mistake of unconsciously *over*compensating for a similar, but *imagined* lack in your child's life. Or you could, just as easily, make sure that your own child ended up failing to fulfill the exact same need that you had yourself.

If there were failings in your own childhood, let go of them. It no longer makes any difference who did or did not do something that may have hurt you or held you back. You are where you are today. You are you! You can, if you choose, take the best of yourself into your role as a parent. It makes good sense to go with the best that you have to give.

If you'd like to be a good parent, then forgiving, accepting, and appreciating your own parents and the other teachers in your past for everything is an exceptional first step.

2. Make the Decision to "Parent"

Many young couples get started raising a family before they ever really make the conscious decision to parent. Just as having a wedding does not automatically make a successful marriage, neither does having children automatically create responsible parents.

To *be* a parent is one thing. To actually *parent* is another. Becoming a parent happens somewhat naturally. Knowing *how* to parent does not.

Making the decision about what to *do* as a parent—in the best way—is saying, "I choose to accept the job of parenting and I make sure that I accept the responsibility to do the job right! I recognize that I am responsible for an important part of my child's well-being."

That is the sort of Self-Talk for parenting you may want to write out on a card and tape to the mirror where you see it every day.

3. Determine Your Objectives

What are your objectives as a parent? What do you really want for your children? Beyond the basics of love, security, happiness, and the other things that almost all parents want to offer, what do you want to give your children?

Most parents would like to bestow a number of values and ideals on their children that will help them deal with life and make the most of it. Do you know what your values and ideals—those that you would like to pass along—are? It will help if you do.

Unless we are consciously aware of what our objectives are as parents, there is all too good a chance that we will let the best of opportunities pass us by.

Write your objectives down. Learning what your parenting objectives are takes only a little time, perhaps some discussion with your spouse, and some thought. The more specific your objectives are, the easier and more naturally you will tend to work at reaching them as you deal with your child on a daily basis.

If you *always* know what your objectives are, the job of parenting should be easier. Your objectives help determine your decisions, and in turn your decisions determine your actions. When a problem or a circumstance comes up, if you have your objectives clearly in mind, you'll have a better chance of knowing what to do about it.

Here is a short sample list of objectives that are typical of what one parent might have for his or her son or daughter. It is not meant to be your list, but it is typical of the kinds of objectives that the consciously aware Predictive Parent sets out to achieve.

Some of the examples on this list are basic. You would probably find them on any good list of parenting objectives. Some of the goals on your list will be different, and more specific—they arise out of a specific relationship or circumstance in life. But for our samples we'll use a list nearly any parent could have written:

PARENTING GOALS—OUR OBJECTIVES FOR OUR CHILDREN AND FOR OURSELVES AS PARENTS

1. *A good home life*

2. *A home where our children will want to spend time*

3. *A good education for each of them—college if possible*

4. *Strong spiritual beliefs that stay with them*

5. *Financial security and an understanding of where financial security comes from*

6. *A spirit of cooperation and mutual understanding*

7. *Open communication between children and parents*

8. *A peaceful, mutually supportive environment in our home*

9. *A sense of personal responsibility and accomplishment*

10. *The ability to share and care about others*

11. *The ability to make decisions for themselves*

12. *Respect for themselves and others*

13. *A strong sense of self-esteem*

14. *Honesty*

15. *The ability to think for themselves*

16. *The ability to tell the difference between right and wrong and have the courage to do what's right*

17. *Friends who will influence them in positive ways*

18. *Happiness*

19. *The ability to say no to bad habits and things that could hurt them*

20. *The determination to not smoke or use harmful drugs, and to be healthy*

21. *Belief in their own capabilities*

22. *The ability to look for and find the good in things*

23. *The ability to love others*

24. *Good relationships and a good family life of their own*

25. *Skills for a good career*

26. *The ability to set goals*

There are many more objectives that could be on your special list. In fact, the more detailed and specific your objectives are, the better they work—because they help you focus your attention on each of them.

As your objectives get more specific, you will also find that they begin to describe specific parenting steps that you expect yourself to take. In the following examples, the objectives themselves are also a step toward the solutions. Here are a few sample objectives—of the more specific kind:

Help Karen see herself as pretty and attractive, especially now while she's wearing her braces.

Let the kids know that we trust them—especially when we are away.

Help Spencer understand that his size and height are just right for him, and that he is perfect to us—and to himself—just the way he is.

Make sure each of the children knows that we are listening and paying attention to each of them individually when it's their turn to talk. Make a special point of listening, being genuinely interested, and responding when we're having a group discussion and when we're at the dinner table.

Encourage creativity. Be supportive (and never critical) of Chris's projects for science class.

I would recommend that you write out a list of parenting objectives for yourself.

Eventually, doing those things that help you reach your objectives becomes a habit—one of the best Predictive Parenting habits you can have.

4. Decide Who Runs the Household

It is often interesting to examine your home life and learn who may actually be running the household. You may want to explore this question for yourself, regarding your own home, and to improve your technique at determining *"who's in charge here?"* Also observe the homes of your friends and other relatives.

Who directly or indirectly controls the decisions that you make and that other people in your home make? How is the time spent, and who most affects who does what and when? Is it you? Your spouse or mate? Is it the children? Is it some other person?

Is your answer consistent with the way you'd like it to be? The decisions you make about who is in charge in your home will have a direct bearing on how effectively you are able to parent.

5. Make the Decision Whether to "Maintain" Children or "Raise Adults"

It is very easy to see the job of parenting as that of "bringing up" children, raising kids instead of raising adults. As one mother put it, "Sometimes I feel like I've lost sight of what my real job of being a parent is. I get so busy feeding, watering, and keeping a roof over their heads for *today* that I forget to get them ready for tomorrow!"

Her "tomorrow" meant her children's futures, of course. And not only did she speak for a lot of parents—she was *right*! We *do* spend so much time and energy just taking care of life today that it seems as though we have little time left to work actively at preparing our children for their futures.

But the real problem is often not with how much time and energy it takes to raise children. In many homes the problem is that there is no conscious recognition of the importance of raising adults—that is, seeing the role of parenting as *preparing* the child to be an adult.

Views on the matter of whether children should be treated as young trainees who are being prepared for adulthood or whether they should be allowed to put the preparation off as long as possible vary greatly from family to family. At times, even two parents within the same family have differing views on how their children should be treated.

Is your position one of believing that children are children—and should be allowed to "act like children"? Or do you feel obliged to be certain that your children begin their preparation, as soon as possible, for the complexities and responsibilities of adulthood that lie ahead? Or do you see your role as being somewhere in between, a parenting role that is dictated by the situation at hand?

There is no "correct" decision, of course. But what you choose, what you decide to do, will have a lot to do with everything else you do that is a part of parenting.

As with each of the key decisions of parenting we are discussing in this chapter, how you see your role as a parent—whether you *provide, maintain,* or *prepare*—will obviously have a lot to do with what you do—and what you say when you talk to your kids, every moment you are in that role.

6. Determine Your Expectations

Be aware of what you expect. If you have already considered what your specific objectives are for your children, that will tell you a lot about what you actually expect from them.

If you expect too *much* of your children, they will fail to reach the mark and give up trying. Or they will end up trying desperately to please you—knowing all along that they can't.

If your expectations are too low, you will pass programming along to them that says, "I don't expect very much of you," which the child unconsciously translates to mean, "I don't believe you are capable."

The best way to avoid the trap of expectations that are

too high or too low is to know what your expectations are. Be aware of your expectations, be fair, and follow them consistently.

Of course, not all expectations have to do with accomplishment. We create expectations about honesty, manners, friends, and many other behaviors and habits. We also have expectations about what our son or daughter can*not* do. At times we even expect and anticipate failure, whether that expectation is warranted or not. And the child will often go one way when our expectations demand that he go another.

The problem is that if our expectations are unrealistic or inconsistent, we will program the child's subconscious with confusion. That leads to indecisiveness, the feeling of inadequacy, and conflicting goals in the child's mind. If the confusing programs are strong enough, we help the child create mental paths that are guaranteed to cause problems in later life.

DO YOU KNOW WHAT YOU EXPECT?

It is not unusual to hear an adult remark, "I just don't know what I want." Many of us have, sometimes quite often, been unsure of ourselves and generally confused about what to do next in our lives.

We stand between two conflicting objectives: One of them is to live up to the expectations that were created for us; the other is to do what we really wanted to do for our *own* reasons. Trying to do it both ways can easily cause us to end up frustrated and unhappy because it is sometimes impossible to follow two paths at one time.

I know adults who will spend the rest of their lives trying to live up to—or *down* to—the expectations their parents created for them. You may have known someone like Don, a man who, in his mid-thirties, still spoke of what his mother had wanted him to be.

Don had not gone on to law school like his mother had hoped he would. He had become a math teacher in a small junior high school instead. And he was still trying to live down the "failure" that not living up to his mother's expectations had created in his life.

In this case the mother had encouraged, and attempted to persuade her son for years, to honor her wish for his future. (Her own father had been a successful attorney.) Don had not wanted to disappoint his mother, but neither had he wanted to become a lawyer.

The result was that Don was never happy in the profession he had chosen for himself either because of the guilt he had created by going against parental expectations. As it turned out, because of misplaced expectations, the man believed he had failed both his mother and himself.

Another man, Sean, had grown up in what he called a generally "negative" home life. As he remembered his childhood, his parents argued most of the time, and they frequently told him not to expect too much out of life.

Not expecting "too much" meant not planning on going to college, not having a good job, not earning more money than was necessary, and not expecting to enjoy a happy home life.

Fortunately, not all of Sean's programming was negative. He had done well enough in school to recognize that he was intelligent and capable. He had had several teachers who had recognized his potential and encouraged him. Sean had also developed the habit of reading books, and some of the biographies he read of successful people had planted the first visions of achievement in his mind.

The result was that Sean was working hard at overcoming the negative programming he got at home, and things were starting to work.

But how much better things might have been for Sean if he had not had first to overcome living *down* to the *negative* expectations of his parents!

LEARNING TO EXPECT WHAT WILL HELP THEM THE MOST

It is easy to expect too little or too much. It is all too common to see parents who try to live their own dreams through the lives of their children—and in so doing expect too much or expect the wrong thing. It is all too often that we see parents who do not believe in their own children enough to expect the best of them. But neither extreme is necessary.

The mother or father who creates unrealistic expectations is *predicting* that the child will not meet them, will rebel or retreat, or will live a life of underlying frustration and unconscious defeat. The parent who creates expectations that hold the child back or nurtures a poor self-image is *predicting* that the child will either struggle to overcome those expectations or, worse yet, will give in to them and accept them as truth.

Look at your own childhood. Look at those times when too much or too little or the wrong things were expected of you. And look at those parts of your childhood that gave you the most encouragement and the greatest chance for fulfillment and happiness. Then look at your own expectations as a parent now. And ask yourself the question, "By my own expectations, what am *I predicting* for the future of my child?"

7. Make the Decision to Be Consistent

One of the surest ways to upset any progress you make as a Predictive Parent is to be inconsistent. Adopting a "style" and not staying with it, or using the style only now and then, doesn't work. Setting rules and then breaking them, as an example, undoes any good that setting the rules might have created in the first place.

In becoming a parent you accept the fact that there are surprises ahead of you. There seem to be plenty of reasons to act one way one day and a different way the next.

In an average week of parenting there are peaks and valleys, times when everything goes according to plan and other times when nothing seems to go right. But what will happen if you allow changes in circumstances to constantly change your methods and rules of parenting?

FEWER "CHANGES" LEAD TO BETTER RESULTS

I know parents who set new rules every week— sometimes more frequently. One couple I know put at least six different "allowance" programs into effect in less than six months! One month the children received fifty cents a day—if they got all of their chores done on time.

Another month they received fifty cents a day only if *all* of them got their chores done; if one of them didn't get his done, none of them got paid. Another month their allowance somehow combined the "One Dollar for Every 'A' on the Report Card" plan, with the "Bonus Dollar for Extra Work Around the House" plan, and none of them was able to figure out who really got what!

Another month the allowances that the parents had forgotten to pay the previous month were rolled into the quarterly savings account with parent contributions. No one was quite sure who lost the most on that one either.

Every thirty days the rules changed. The only thing the kids could rely on was the assurance that in a few weeks the rules would change again and it would be a whole new game. And unfortunately, that is exactly how the kids saw their allowance program—as a game, played unfairly at best, and managed by the *same* parents who were trying to teach them how to manage their money and their futures!

Most of the inconsistencies of parenting, however, are not nearly so obvious as an unsteady allowance plan. I have met parents who at one time will punish their children for staying out past curfew and at other times ignore the curfew completely. There are times when a child's behavior may be rewarded one moment and the same behavior is criticized the next.

There is a reason that this kind of inconsistency upsets the best of good intentions. Mixed signals, fed to the unconscious mind, create mental programs that are unclear, and confusing. If the programs that operate the young person's mental computer are full of contradictions, how can that boy or girl ever set solid, clear directions through life?

CLEAR DIRECTIONS CREATE CLEAR PROGRAMS

Contradictory or inconsistent programs in a young person's subconscious mind cause no end of problems for both the child and the parent. And most of the time neither the child nor the parent has the slightest idea what the *real* reason for the problem actually is! Part of the child's program tells him one thing, another part tells him to do something else.

If we gave directions like that to the computer that guides a rocket into space, it would never get off the ground.

By unknowingly giving our own children inconsistent programs, we literally program them for misdirection. Certainly we must believe that the best of the guidance we choose to use in our parenting deserves to be used and followed consistently.

Our new awareness of the programming requirements of the human brain has shown us why consistency is so important. We now know, for instance, that the brain responds *best* to its strongest and clearest programs. It reacts most directly and most naturally to those programs that are uncomplicated and unquestioned.

We have known for years the positive benefits of being reliable. But we now know that being reliable is not only beneficial—it is *essential* to creating good, solid, positive programs in young people. Being consistent, and thereby creating strong, consistent programs, is a basic necessity for the future well-being of every child.

When I talk to a parent who says, "I'm always consistent with my child," I know that parent is also saying, "The programs I give my child are strong and consistent."

This does not mean that there should not be exceptions. There are times when a rule must be broken, a mistake overlooked, or there is a special circumstance that requires special handling. But there can be consistency even in those. It takes only a moment of self-evaluation to know if you are typically consistent with your parenting or not.

If you have not been as consistent as you could have been in the past, I hope that you will recognize how important your ongoing consistency is to the future of your child.

Those of us who have been inconsistent have been so because of our *own* programming. Being consistent, like all behavior, is a habit that is learned—it is a part of the conditioning we received as children.

8. Make the Decision to Practice Predictive Parenting

It is a lot easier to succeed at something when you are aware that you are doing it. The more aware you are, the more *decisive* you are, about everything you do as a parent, the greater your chances of success will be.

The first step toward being conscious of your parenting is to make a clear, conscious decision to parent every day in the most positive, predictive way possible.

If you share your parenting responsibilities with a spouse or some other cooperative adult, discuss this and the previous parenting decisions with him or her. Ask yourself, and each other, how you feel about each of them.

These decisions are too important to "sort of" decide where you stand on each of them. Of the dozens of decisions you could make about parenting, these few are some of the most important because they are decisions that directly affect how you will, consciously or unconsciously, program your child.

KNOW—IN ADVANCE—WHERE YOU STAND

The decisions that we have discussed here will set the tone for nearly every other parenting decision you make in the future. If you decide now where you stand on each of them, the day-to-day decisions that follow should be easier. You will have already decided—*in advance*—where you stand.

How you parent may appear to be "natural." But the best parenting is seldom the result of unconscious acceptance of someone else's style or rules. Predictive Parenting is the result of your own conscious choices—your personal decisions about how and why you choose to parent as you do.

Ask yourself how you have used these choices in the past and how you might reevaluate and put to work the same parenting decisions in the future.

The more you're aware of how you feel about each of these decisions, the more *you* will be in control of the programs you type into your child's mental computer. That programming should never be left up to chance—and you can make sure that it isn't.

Chapter 7

The Rule of Personal Responsibility

There are two ingredients at the root of every success or happiness each of us will ever have and at the heart of every lasting individual achievement. If we do not have enough of them, our chances for success and fulfillment are slim. If we have them in abundance, our chances for living a worthwhile life are almost assured.

They are the twin skills of *Personal Responsibility* and *Self-esteem*. Even love, as essential as it is to our lives, and no matter how much of it we receive, can never take the place of personal responsibility and self-esteem. These two nearly magical qualities work together to manifest the very best of our nature.

Each of these skills builds the other. The teaching of personal responsibility leads to the building of self-esteem. And the building of self-esteem leads to the development of personal responsibility.

If you understand the nature and the source of these two qualities of personal growth and if you learn how to teach these skills to your children, you will have taken advantage of one of the greatest tools of Predictive Parenting. You will also create a solid base for parenting, on which, along with love, all other worthwhile parenting can grow.

THE PRIMARY PROGRAMS OF THE SUBCONSCIOUS MIND

In the programming process of the human mind, some of our subconscious programs are more powerful than others. These are called Primary Programs because they affect all of the other programs we receive. Our Primary Programs establish our basic direction, our underlying beliefs, and our strongest overall attitudes and perspectives on life.

An example of a Primary Program is our sense of *personal integrity,* which governs the role that truth and honesty play in our life. Another is our sense of *personal strength,* which governs the level of courage we feel inside when problems confront us.

When it comes to a confrontation between one program and another, the Primary Program always wins out. If, for instance, your child has become conditioned to have a high level of personal integrity, later attempts to encourage him to be dishonest will fail or will not last. The child may tell a lie, but his Primary Program will do everything it can to get him back on track and back into being truthful.

If, instead, a child has become conditioned to have a low level of personal integrity, then that will become a Primary Program that will work to convince the child that the truth is not important and that it's okay to avoid it. That Primary Program will win out if a lesser program tries to convince the child that he should tell the truth.

It is in this way that each of our Primary Programs ends up having an incredible amount of influence in our lives. Primary Programs are some of the earliest programs we receive and they are some of the strongest programs we receive. The result is that these Primary Programs end up affecting, influencing, or in some cases even modifying or changing other programs we receive.

Two of our strongest Primary Programs are the programs of *personal responsibility* and *self-esteem*. And that is why these two skills—these two Primary Programs—have the influence in our lives that they do. Personal responsibility and self-esteem are "skills" because they are taught and they are learned. And they are Primary Programs because they direct, or in some way affect, almost everything about us.

Each of us has only a few of these extra-strength Primary Programs. But, as you might imagine, they are among the most important programs we will ever have—*and we receive each of them from someone else!* We were not born with any of them; we *learned* them. They are conditioned, taught to us by our parents or by whoever had enough influence in our lives to unconsciously convince us to accept the teaching—the programs—they were giving us.

TEACHING THE RULE OF PERSONAL RESPONSIBILITY

The *Rule of Personal Responsibility* is:
Each individual is always responsible for his or her own actions.

That means that you, as an adult, are responsible for every one of your actions. It also means that your children are also responsible for *their* actions.

The simplicity of that rule should not suggest that the rule is not important. It is simple, but it is important—exceptionally important!

A newborn infant, of course, cannot be held accountable for doing something "right" or "wrong." When do we begin to let young people know that what they do, creates much of what happens *to* them? How early in life, and to what extent, should we let children know that, like it or not, aware or not, they are already responsible?

There is a broad difference of opinions as to when exactly we are accountable for what we do. *The best rule to follow is to assume accountability as early (or as young) as possible.*

If you teach responsibility and accountability early in a child's life, the child will more naturally grow up recognizing that he plays the leading role in determining the consequences in his own future.

If you wait until your child is fully accountable before beginning to teach him full accountability, he will not learn it as easily or as naturally. That's because his previous programming has already begun to convince him that he does not have to be fully responsible for each of his own actions.

Since the subconscious mind accepts whatever it is programmed with often enough and strongly enough, the child, when he refuses to recognize that *he is responsible,* is simply acting on the program that he *believes* to be true.

Because of his inaccurate program, he has no other choice—at least none that he is aware of. He honestly believes that someone *else* is responsible, or that the world is at fault! He believes that what happens to him is not really up to him.

As an example, let's take two different families. In each of them a six-year-old son is told that he has to clean up his room before he can go to a movie. In one family the Rule of Personal Responsibility is taught and adhered to.

75

In the other family there is no clear understanding or teaching of the Rule of Personal Responsibility. So it is seldom used, used improperly, or generally not adhered to.

The first boy knows that by *not* cleaning his room, *he himself is making the decision* that he cannot go to the movie. He recognizes his role, his responsibility in the matter, and he understands his own accountability—the consequence being that he does not get to go.

Whether he likes it or not (or even agrees with the idea or not), he knows that *he*—not his parents or someone else—but *his own actions,* and therefore his own *choice,* has determined that he is not going to the movie.

In the second household the young boy also does not clean his room and because of this also does not get to go to the movie. But in this case the boy is not even *aware* that *he* made the decision himself! He blames his parents for not letting him go instead of recognizing *who* is really responsible.

The fact is that the second boy *is* responsible for his own actions. He just doesn't realize that yet. As a result, he doesn't make the *connection* between his actions and the results.

Imagine if, in the above example, the boy who did not understand the Rule of Personal Responsibility had been told, "We are going to the movie. You can go with us if you straighten your room first. *It is your choice."*

If that boy were taught the real meaning of the words *it is your choice,* he would, in time, begin to understand that the choice is his—and so is the responsibility.

All too often a parent will say something like, "That's what you get! You didn't fix the bike tire when I told you to, and I'm not going to give you a ride," or, "I told you to be in by ten-thirty and you were an hour late. You're not going out this weekend," or, "You knew what would happen to you if you didn't get your math assignment done on time."

Teaching kids the Rule of Personal Responsibility every time the opportunity comes up is the best way the rule can be taught. What's missing from the parents' comments in the preceding examples? The important message that says, *"You choose!"*

Let your kids know that *they, not you,* ultimately decide if things work for them or if they don't. It might seem at times that the deck is stacked, that there is nothing they can do that works right. But almost everything that happens *to* us is affected or changed by what *we do.* In time, if you teach the Rule of Personal Responsibility and stay with it, that message gets through.

Unfortunately, when we become adults, unless we learn better, we also, at times, fail to make the connection. For some of us, not learning that rule ourselves has caused problems for us too. Long after we became adults and would have gladly followed the rule, some of us had never been shown what an understanding of personal responsibility could do for us.

A RULE THAT AFFECTS EACH OF US EVERY DAY

If we oversleep, for example, and arrive late for work as a result, it is easy to blame someone else for not waking us up. But who is actually responsible? Almost anyone over the age of seven or so years old can set an alarm clock or find a way to get up on time if he has to.

Every day in school, teachers hear excuses from students who did not get their homework done on time because those students have not yet learned the Rule of Personal Responsibility. The result is the students shift the blame to anything and everything else rather than

77

knowing that failure to get homework done on time is, in most cases, the direct result of having failed to take the personal responsibility to do it.

It seems as if this should be easy enough for almost anyone to understand. After all, it is logical. When we do things "right," they tend to work out better for us. When we fail to do what we *should* do, we usually have to pay the price. We all know that. There is no mystery to it at all. Yet many of us, even as adults, repeatedly overlook the Rule of Personal Responsibility.

Teaching the Rule of Personal Responsibility in simple, everyday ways *throughout* childhood can create a positive internal program that may do as much for that child's future as any other training or education he will ever receive.

Think of what hardships our failure to accept responsibility can cause in our own lives. It could be said that it is the failure to understand and accept personal responsibility that is, in itself, responsible for more of our personal problems than any other failing we might act out from the internal programs that guide us.

We, not someone else, make most of the decisions about what happens *to* us in life. We personally set a chain reaction of events in motion by what we *do* and by what we do *not* do. Most of the excuses we will ever come up with for the problems that have troubled us have been nothing more than the predictable results of our own actions.

We are not talking here of the things that are clearly out of our personal control. Unfortunately, the less we understand the Rule of Personal Responsibility, the more we tend to believe that something or someone *else* is *always* in control—and that we are not.

The less we recognize the direct cause-and-effect relationship between what we do or do not do and what happens to us, the more likely we are to believe that there are *external* forces at work, outside of our control, that are somehow designed to make things work against us.

THE POSITIVE BENEFITS OF PERSONAL RESPONSIBILITY

The reason for learning this rule is not only to avoid problems, of course. The rule works both ways. When you do things *right,* or in a way that works for you, you are also creating the *benefits* that come your way as a result.

Taking personal responsibility for ourselves is part of the basic foundation of every part of "well-being" that we create in life. But it goes even beyond that.

If a young person has not learned to take responsibility for himself, he will not feel he *deserves* the rewards that come to him.

When you meet someone who cannot accept a compliment, for example, or someone who is always belittling himself, along with some other subconscious programming problems he may have you can be sure that that person has not learned the Rule of Personal Responsibility. How can we reach and accept any kind of success if we do not feel that we are responsible for that success—or anything else that is a positive part of who we are?

All too often we avoid accepting our own personal responsibility and choice in even the most natural, day-to-day decisions we make. We frequently hear someone make a comment to someone else such as, "You look great in that dress. Is it new?" only to hear the answer, "Oh, it's just something I had hanging in the closet." The real answer *should* have been the *truth:* "Thank you. I just bought it yesterday, and I like it too!"

It is the Rule of Personal Responsibility that directs

most of our actions throughout life—regardless of who we are or what we do in life.

What each of us learns about responsibility, in our youth, always affects the future that is in front of us. But the Rule of Personal Responsibility goes beyond what it teaches young people for the far-distant future. It affects every part of how they look at—and deal with—every day of their growing-up years.

The reason the Rule of Personal Responsibility is so important to understand as a part of parenting is that without it even the best programs we can give our children will fail to work as well as they should.

WHAT CAN WE DO NOW?

It can be difficult to teach a skill to a child when it is a skill we did not learn very well ourselves. What should we do now if the Primary Programs of personal responsibility and self-esteem we received were less than the best?

If that is the case, the first thing to do is to be honest about it and recognize the fact that our own programming may need some improvement.

The next decision is to learn how to create better Primary Programs of personal responsibility in our children.

The best way to get started is with a Predictive Parent's look at an incredibly essential part of our lives—*self-esteem*.

Chapter 8

A Predictive Parenting Look at Self-esteem

In many respects, everything that we are doing to help give our children a better picture of themselves, we are doing—almost entirely—to build their *self-esteem*.

The development of healthy self-esteem in your child is the underlying objective of all Predictive Parenting. The creation of self-esteem is the primary purpose for our learning to talk to our children in a better way.

That raises self-esteem to a pretty high level of importance, and it is well deserved. Self-esteem is a quality of mind that can never be overemphasized or overstated. It is so *vitally* important to the mind of a young person that any amount of it we can give them is worth every effort that it takes.

A child can never get too *much* self-esteem. Few of them will ever have as much as they could use.

When I have discussed the importance of self-esteem on radio and television shows, I invariably receive a call from a listener or a viewer who asks the question, "If I give my son too *much* self-esteem, won't he think he's *too* good?"

True self-esteem doesn't work that way. In fact, strong

self-esteem creates the *opposite* of a "me first" attitude. Your child will always base his picture of life on the picture that he has of himself. The more your child likes himself or herself, the better he or she will like others. The greater the value he places on himself, the greater the value he will place on everything else around him.

Children with *low* self-esteem try to pretend that they are more important than they actually feel they are. Children with *high* self-esteem have no need to put themselves above others. They're happy with who *they* are, and they do everything they can to help *other* children see themselves in the same way.

THE EXCEPTIONAL VALUE OF SELF-ESTEEM

Why is self-esteem so important? What is it about self-esteem that places it above any other quality (except perhaps our own spiritual beliefs) that we can ever teach our children? What is self-esteem—and what does it do that is so important to the life of a child?

To many, the term *self-esteem* means to love one's self—and that *is* an accurate description. But the meaning of self-esteem that we are using here is "self-*value*." That includes love, caring, and belief, but most importantly it recognizes that self-esteem is the *value* that each of us places on our selves and on the role each of us plays in our own lives.

For many, there is some confusion about this concept of caring for our selves—whether or not it is really okay to like our *selves* that much, or whether self-love is somehow self-centered or a form of narcissism. Self-esteem—self-value—is not like that at all.

When we understand what self-esteem is and the role that it plays in the mental health and the life of a child, we begin to understand that the only thing that could be *wrong* with self-esteem is not having enough of it.

Self-esteem is, and always will be, one of the most *helpful* and most necessary parts of who a child is—and a principal part of why they do what they do, how they see others, and how they live out their lives—long after they have left childhood behind.

WHAT SELF-ESTEEM TOUCHES IN A YOUNG PERSON'S LIFE

One of the best ways to understand the importance of self-esteem for a young person is to look at what areas of their lives self-esteem touches or affects. Some time ago I began to take note of the specific areas in a child's or young person's life that self-esteem was *directly* affecting.

In time I recognized that success in life is always tied to self-esteem—how much or how little a person has.

Here are some of the areas in the life of a child that are directly affected by his or her self-esteem. As you read through this list, ask yourself, "Does my child's self-esteem affect *this* in his or her life?"

It is interesting to note that what self-esteem touches in all of these areas, in one way or another, affects *all* of us. For your child, in some way, every day, his or her *self-esteem* affects his or her:

Attitude
Happiness
Initiative

Enthusiasm
Temperament
Productivity
Energy
Creativity
Problem handling
Spirit
Determination
Expectations
Openness
Learning
Patience
Responsibility
Health
Physical appearance
Schoolwork
Getting along with others
Posture
Speech
Attentiveness
Memory
Concentration
Sense of personal responsibility
Acceptance of criticism
Self-confidence
Anxiety and stress
Security
Courage
Honesty
Moods
Follow-through
Trust
Character
Sensitivity
Habits
Honor
Values

The effect of self-esteem on every one of these areas of a young person's life is remarkable.

To find out just how important self-esteem *is* in all those important areas, let's select just a few of the areas on the list and find out what role, self-esteem plays in each of them.

ATTITUDE

How a child feels about himself—at *any* time—will *always* affect his attitude. Children with a strong sense of self-esteem consistently have a better attitude about things than children whose self-esteem is injured or lacking.

A child's attitudes about anything—school, friends, home, parents, responsibilities—are *always* tied directly to the value he places on himself. The higher the value he recognizes in himself, the higher the value he will place on the other things in his life.

HEALTH

How can a young person be expected to respect the importance of his personal health—what he does with his physical self—if he does not first respect his internal self, the picture of himself that he has stored in the files of his mind? The self-esteem that a young person carries with him will affect nearly every choice he makes about the body he lives in.

Doctors and therapists who have to deal with young-sters who abuse themselves with drugs or alcohol, for example, know this all too well. Taking care of oneself physically always follows one's mental and emotional care. And that is a product of self-esteem.

A strong sense of self-worth creates a self-identity that wants to function at its best! The mind of someone with strong self-esteem says, "I like who I am and I like the body I'm living in. I choose to treat myself right because I deserve to be treated right. *I deserve it and I am worth it.*"

HONESTY

High self-esteem fosters high self-expectations of honesty and integrity. Low self-esteem creates the belief that it's okay to step over the line.

The mind says, "If I don't care about *myself,* why should I care about what anyone else cares or thinks?" "If I don't value my own truth, why should I value someone else's truth?" "I'm not important! Why should I think that honesty is important?"

A young person who sees himself or herself as having worth places the same high worth or value on everything he or she says or does.

GETTING ALONG WITH OTHERS

It is impossible to get along with others if you can't get along with yourself. It is impossible for a child or a young person to genuinely believe in and like others when he or she does not believe in or like himself or herself. The better a child feels about himself, the better he will feel about the people around him.

SCHOOLWORK

The mind of a child who does not value himself says, "Why bother? What difference does it make?" And to that person, to that mind, it doesn't make any difference whether he does well in school or not! What is the purpose? Especially when that same mind tells the child, "You're not capable of doing well—and even if you were capable, why try?"

Countless parents and teachers have told me that "for some reason this child or that student just won't try, won't apply himself, won't make the effort." Why? *Because that child or student doesn't believe he has enough value to make it worth it.* The value a child places on his schoolwork is always affected by the value he places on himself first.

The mind of a child who has a good sense of self sees things differently. That mind says, "I'm important, and I like doing my best!" You can't expect any more from a child than the best that he expects from himself.

HABITS

Developing good habits takes purpose. And purpose requires that there be an internal reason to develop the good habit. If a child sees himself as being unworthy, he finds it almost impossible to develop worthwhile habits.

That affects his dress, his room, how he spends his time, the friends he chooses, how he treats himself and others, how he talks, how he thinks, and a host of other skills that are the results of the habits he has created for himself.

The bedrock that all positive habits are built on is self-esteem. If the child's self-esteem is high, his habits—the way he lives—will be habits that help him live up to the image of himself that he has in his mind.

If his self-esteem is low, he will live down to the picture that his own internal files have created for him.

We always live "up to" or "down to" the picture of ourselves that we believe most about ourselves.

Those examples give us a picture of how all-encompassing self-esteem is in its influence in a young person's life. Self-esteem does indeed touch everything.

It is no wonder, then, that a lack of self-value and self-respect should create such problems for a young person. Quite a few of the items on that list are vital to a workable, manageable life—every day.

THE TRAGIC RESULTS OF INJURED SELF-ESTEEM

We have all seen the effects of low self-esteem. It is always unfortunate; it is sometimes disastrous.

How can a young boy who, at this very moment, is living in a small apartment in a back alley of the worst part of the ghetto ever hope to live his life to its fullest when he is beginning to believe that he is not as good as someone else?

What about the young girl who is growing up in a middle-class home and has learned to believe that she is unattractive or that she doesn't measure up to her parents' expectations? Her own poor self-worth will take its toll in ways that will almost guarantee problems and unhappiness in her future.

We have all known people who were qualified and capable but who failed to meet any of their important goals in life *because their self-esteem wasn't high enough to help them get where they wanted to go.*

We prepare ourselves to succeed only when we learn to place a high value on who we are *inside,* and a high value on ourselves as individuals. How well we *like* ourselves determines, for each of us, just how high that potential really is.

Self-esteem—or the lack of it—is not governed by heredity, intelligence, education, wealth, social standing, or luck. Self-esteem, for each of us, is governed by our programming—what we *learn* to believe about ourselves. Because self-esteem is learned, it can be taught. And as parents or teachers, teaching it is up to each of us.

Chapter 9

A Predictive Parenting Program for Building Self-esteem

Most of our early self-esteem came to us from two sources. The first of these was in the positive messages about our *selves* that we received from others.

What we heard may not always have sounded like praise, but anything we heard from someone else that told us we were doing well, created positive beliefs about ourselves.

Our other early source of self-esteem came from ourselves and it was built on our own behavior; when we did something that we were proud of, we built more self-esteem—we increased our *value* to our *self*.

These two self-esteem sources worked hand-in-hand. When we did something well, we felt good about ourselves. That in turn made us want to do more of the same. So we did something else well, felt good about it, received approval, and laid another brick in our foundation of self-esteem.

You might remember a time when that happened to you. It may have been a huge accomplishment, with praise to match, or it may have been a simple task and a few simple words of approval. But the effect was the same: You felt *better* about yourself because of it.

There were other times when our early self-esteem was created almost without notice—the results were there, but they may not have been obvious at the time. These were the times when we did something we were proud of, but the only reward we received was from us to ourselves.

When a child does something he would like to be proud of, he will unconsciously reward himself or shrug his accomplishment off, based on the level of self-worth that has already been created in his mind. Our self-esteem always *builds* on whatever *earlier* self-esteem we have built up in the past.

THE *FUTURE* THAT SELF-ESTEEM CREATES

When I was young, I worked during the summer with several teenage friends bailing and stacking hay on a farm near the town where I lived. The days were long and hot, and the bales of hay weighed seventy or eighty pounds each. We had to lift the bales above our heads to get them to the top of the stack, and it was back-breaking work.

As we worked, I noticed that some of my friends were going about the job with enthusiasm—to them it was a challenge and the hard work was less important than the goal of getting the job done right. But a few of the others saw things differently. Each bale they lifted was an effort—and whether they did a good job meant nothing at all. Their only goal was quitting time.

I could not help but wonder what the difference was between the two kinds of friends. Some of them were proud of their accomplishment and some of them were not. I did not know then that some of them placed a value on their work because they had already placed a value on *themselves*.

I thought about that job years later, when I ran into some of those same friends. I should not have been at all surprised. Without exception, those of my friends who had worked hard to do it right had gone on to become successful in their lives. Those who were only waiting for "quitting time" had done very little with their lives.

What made the difference? The difference that affected and directed their lives was the difference that each of them had in his sense of *self*. Years ago the job was stacking hay. Today the job is living life in a way that has value and worth. Some of them are still getting the job done right. Some of them are still waiting for quitting time.

GOLD STARS OF SELF-WORTH

Why do some children develop an early sense of self-esteem when other children do not? For some of us, if we were fortunate, someone who cared sat down and told us some of those wonderful things we wanted—and needed—to hear about ourselves.

They may have told us what a great life we had in front of us, or how smart we were, or how good we were at some thing or another, or how special we were. I know elderly people who can still remember when someone, fifty or sixty years ago, told them something like that. They never forgot it. It was that important.

As we grew older, the self-esteem in each of us was shaped and formed. Some of us got a lot. Some of us seemed to get passed over and ended up with very little.

Some young people—at the age of ten or twelve—already seem to have gotten enough self-esteem stored up to last them a lifetime. They are fortunate.

Other people, with most of their lives behind them, are *still* looking for some good news about themselves. And they're not having much luck finding it.

As adults, that can be a difficult side of life to deal with. Think for a moment about how self-esteem is formed.

You get a gold star for something you did right, so you do something right again and get another gold star—and then another and another. You may see the gold star pasted on the bulletin board or in a report card, but *it is the gold stars that are in your mind that count.* Some children grow up without any gold stars in their mind.

HOW MUCH SELF-ESTEEM WOULD *YOU* LIKE TO HAVE?

Just imagine what we could do, as adults, with an undefeatable sense of self! Imagine the confidence we would have. With a strong enough sense of *self,* there is nothing that we could not do that we honestly believe we should be able to achieve.

At seminars and lectures I have conducted I have met intelligent, capable, potentially unlimited men and women who told me that they can't get the job they want because they are not *assertive* enough! I have met people who told me that they wasted *years* going in the wrong direction because they didn't have the fortitude to make the right decision.

I have known fine, clear-thinking individuals who stopped their goals short of the risk—because the picture of themselves that they carried around in their heads didn't measure up to the challenge.

Was it their capability? Of course not. Was it their

intelligence or education? Almost never. It was their failing sense of self-esteem, given to them as children, and dictating poor choices through life—choices they would *never* have made had their own self-esteem aimed them in a better direction.

HOW DO YOU REWARD THE "SELF" IN YOUR KIDS?

I wonder sometimes how many of us who are now parents really remember how important it is to give gold stars to the children in our lives. It doesn't have to be an award for doing something right—some of the most important stars are those that we give our children just for being the incredible young human beings that they are! They can never get too many of them, and all too many children get so few of them!

What are you doing and saying *now* to make sure your child will have enough self-esteem to get him through and help him make it to the top of his potential? What insurance are you giving him?

Ask yourself the questions, "What do I really say when I talk to my kids? What do they hear *in their minds* when I talk to them now?" Do your words paint the pictures that you would like to put into the files in their minds? They need those pictures—just like you and I needed them when we were young; we *still* need them!

As adults we have learned that there is no "happily ever after." The real life we face each day isn't the same as the closing scenes of a movie that ends with a rose-colored sunset. Tomorrow morning we have to get up and face life all over again—and so do our kids.

And for your kids, what you say to them tomorrow, and

each day thereafter, could, if you choose, fortify their young minds with more "strength of self."

If you don't choose, you will leave them to their own resources, to make it on their own, with nothing more than more of the same kinds of files that they already have in their minds—whatever those files may hold.

THE MORE YOU GIVE, THE BETTER THEY DO

Your children need all the self-esteem you can give them. There will be enough hazards along the way in life that will try to take away any self-esteem they have already stored up.

Unless a child's self-esteem is so strong that nothing can counteract it, every error, every mistake, every bad grade, every reprimand, every negative remark from a parent, and every step over the line of "right and wrong" will attack that self-esteem.

I talked recently with a group of schoolchildren who were discussing self-esteem. We were talking about the value that each of us has, when Eric, an eleven-year-old, summed up the frustration many children face, when he said, "If I'm so good, why does my dad always *yell* at me?"

Eric was working hard to have a good opinion of himself. But the "good" opinion of himself was having a hard time coping with a far different message he was getting from his father. It is possible that Eric's dad has a great opinion of Eric. He just hasn't figured out how to let Eric know it yet.

The value of strong *self*-value in the mind of a child is beyond question. Helping our children get enough of it is essential. If you conscientiously practice Predictive Parenting, you give yourself an advantage. You know that what you say—everything you say—has an effect. You know that the words you use affect your child's day today, and his future.

In time, the pattern of self-esteem we create in our child's mind will take off on its own. It will follow the pattern we give it and begin to build itself. Given the right words of self-belief to follow, our child's mind will take those words in and *duplicate* them on its own. Once they do that, we can relax. The youngster will be off and running. We will have given our son or daughter one of the best tools we know to give.

A PRACTICAL PROGRAM FOR BUILDING SELF-ESTEEM

The building of self-esteem in a child is not an overnight process. But there *are* some ways to make sure you are doing everything you can to help.

The following steps are not only essential, they will help you stay on top of doing something about the self-esteem that your child is developing in his or her young mind *right now:*

1. Tell Your Child Something Good About Himself or Herself Every Day.

This can be something as simple as saying, "I like the way you talk to people" or "That's a talent I wish I had" or "You can be proud of that." And it doesn't take a major pronouncement to communicate your approval. In most cases, even an offhand comment will do. In other cases, sit the young person down, look him right in the eye, and tell him about it. And a lot of hugs and even an occasional handshake can help you get the point across.

Faithfully practicing finding some positive quality to *recognize* in each young person each day creates, for you, a habit of actively helping to build self-esteem. The quality that you mention can be a skill or even the yet-to-come promise of a skill. Or what you show your young person of himself or herself can be a talent of any kind, an attitude, an accomplishment, or even a few well-chosen words such as, "You're important, just because you're *you*."

A young person's garden of self-esteem does not spring up overnight from the planting of a few seeds and an occasional shower. It takes careful planting, the best nurturing you can give it, and watering every day.

2. Set Simple, Short-Term Daily or Weekly Goals That Your Children *Can* Meet, and Give Them the *Encouragement* They Need to Help Them Reach Each Goal.

Goal setting works best when the goals are practical and attainable and when the goals are set and reviewed on a consistent basis. When you take the time to structure positive goals with a young person, you create the opportunity to recognize the *success* of reaching them— and *successful achievement of a worthwhile goal always adds to self-esteem.*

Positive goals can be set for just about anything. But it is the fact that the goal was set in the *first* place that makes the accomplishment more rewarding.

For example, here are several "tasks" that eleven-year-old Marie will be expected to accomplish at home during a particular school week: clean and rearrange her closet, including the doll shelf, write a thank-you note to Aunt Margaret for the birthday gift, set the dinner table on Tuesday and Thursday, finish folding the rest of her clothes and putting them in her dresser, and practice piano for at least forty-five minutes before her piano lesson on Wednesday.

Each of these minor responsibilities could come and go almost without notice; they're usually noticed only if they're *not* completed.

But if Marie's mom or dad takes the time to write each of these responsibilities down on a goal card and tacks it to Marie's bulletin board and, along with Marie, checks off each goal after it is accomplished, a lot more will have been achieved than the accomplishment of the goal itself. Marie will *sense* the accomplishment!

It is the *recognition* of the accomplishment that will build Marie's self-esteem. In this example, the parents' objective is not only to help Marie learn the skill of setting goals (an important skill to learn in itself). The objective is to use those same "tasks" as self-esteem builders. Doing that takes almost no extra time for Marie's parents. It is a Predictive Parenting opportunity in which the rewards strongly outweigh the cost.

3. Award Their Accomplishments, Especially the Small Accomplishments.

Awarding young people for their accomplishments (including those that were not set as goals) is another self-esteem builder that creates strong positive programs in the filing center of a young person's mind.

It is interesting to compare how often a parent will reprimand or punish a young person for doing something wrong with how often that same parent will *reward* the young person for doing something *right*.

In any given day or week of your parenting life, do the punishments you give for failure outweigh the acknowledgments you give for success? Do the rewards you give surpass the reprimands you pass out?

If the answer is that your youngster doesn't do enough things right to *deserve* the rewards, reconsider: Almost any young person, with positive encouragement, will do enough things right to deserve attention and reward.

Remember, your positive recognition of almost *anything,* accomplished *or* attempted, *will add another program file of self-esteem in a child's mind.*

4. Every Time You Talk to Your Child, Ask Yourself the Question, "Am I Building Self-esteem?"

In time, the process of helping a young person build self-esteem becomes as automatic and as natural as breathing or smiling or caring.

Getting started begins with thinking about self-esteem consciously and working actively to create it. But in time the "process" becomes more natural; the positive growth of the young person's self-esteem becomes as natural and as ordinary as growing up.

If you were to start with nothing more than the six steps that are outlined here and read them to yourself even once a week for the next few months, you would almost automatically create the habit of teaching and building self-esteem.

By learning to build self-esteem, at every opportunity and without fail, you will be giving your children an advantage in life, which, unfortunately, many others will never have.

5. Write the Words "I Build Self-esteem" on a Card and Tape It to the Mirror Where You Will See It Each Morning.

This is perhaps the easiest self-esteem-building step you can take—and it may be the most important. It is your own *decision* to build self-esteem that will precede every other action you will take in developing self-esteem in the young people in your life.

The purpose of this step is not only to remind you to build self-esteem each day. It is to remind you of your responsibility as a parent or teacher. If there is a young person in your life, it is your responsibility to add to that young person's self-esteem. That is a natural responsibility of being an adult.

Some adults never realize this or figure it out. Some of them realize it but never do anything about it. And some adults—those who recognize their responsibility and take action—help create positive young minds and future adults for whom self-esteem will be a natural part of life.

Writing the words *"I Build Self-esteem"* on a card and posting the card on your dressing-room mirror will not get the job done all by itself, but it is a significant starting step. Whether you are already an active self-esteem builder or just getting started, *write the words.*

As we have learned, it is our own internal *programming* that controls *our* behavior. If you want to build self-esteem in your children, give your*self* a clear and simple program that will help you get the job done: *I build self-esteem.*

6. Teach Your Children About Self-esteem. Let Them Know Why It's Important and How to Get It.

Let your kids in on *what* you're doing and *why* you're doing it. The more they understand, even at a young age, that we live out the pictures of ourselves that we put in our minds—and how those pictures get there—the better equipped they will be to help build self-esteem for themselves.

No young person, at any age, learns everything about self-esteem in one day. Understanding self-esteem takes practice. It is something we "feel" as much as understand. It is something that grows within us; each time we do something that builds it, we feel it a little bit more. Each time we do something that takes some of it away, we feel that it is gone.

Children like stories. Give them examples from your own experience, and from theirs, about the times when self-esteem was created—and when it wasn't. Talk to them about their friends and their friends' self-esteem.

Even at an early age most kids begin to understand. They, too, see the world around them. They see what works and what doesn't. They even know when other kids their own age are succeeding or failing. You can help them understand *why*.

LEARN TO OVERRIDE FRUSTRATION WITH BELIEF

When I am working with a parent who hopes for the best for a young person but isn't sure what to expect, I am often reminded of the saying "Learn to expect the best—but don't expect a miracle."

I suspect we would all fare a little better if we *did* expect a few more miracles now and then. But as parents, we also have to be practical. Teaching self-esteem takes a lot of time and a lot of belief. Without taking the time to build self-esteem, we cannot possibly build it. Without *believing* in a positive outcome, we simply stop trying.

When you are doing your best to build self-esteem in your children, don't give up. The creation of self-esteem is a labor of love. It will always take as much time as you can give it, and more. And it will always demand the best of your belief. But when you know that it is a young person's *self-esteem* that will direct *every other belief and behavior* that young person will ever have, the creation of a clear, strong sense of self-worth in your child is worth all the love you put into it.

THE MOST IMPORTANT THING YOU CAN DO

Those suggestions look simple enough; and if you want them to *work,* they *should* be simple. Helping your child develop self-esteem should not be a chore; it should be a way of life.

If you want to avoid some of the pitfalls of parenting, and if you want to ensure more future success for your children, start *first* with building self-esteem.

Most of us who are parents today are concerned about the influences and problems our children face. But if you were to ask me today, "What is the most important thing I can do, right now, to make sure my son or daughter will come through it all—and make it through in good shape?" My answer would be simple:

*If you want to give your children their **best,** give them self-esteem.*

If I had only one gift I could give to my children, and to yours, it would be the gift of self-esteem. There is no child who does not benefit from the *value* that is created within him.

There is no star that shines brighter, than the star of a child who believes in himself.

Chapter 10

What *Not* to Say When You Talk to Your Kids

The process of positive Predictive Parenting goes far beyond what you say when you talk to your kids. But when you talk to them, what *do* you say?

You are probably not going to put this book down, run into your youngster's room, and suddenly announce to him that he is wonderful and marvelous just like that!— although doing that may not be a bad idea.

For many of us, our present relationships with our kids aren't built on surprise exclamations of that kind.

When we actually get down to the business of what to say, what not to say, what to add, and what to avoid, there are some examples that will help.

The first examples we will look at are those things that we may have said in the past—and we've now learned that we're better off never saying them at all. Some of those situations that we have run into in the past could, in the future, benefit from knowing what *not* to say the next time a similar situation comes up.

After practicing Predictive Parenting for even a few weeks, many parents have told me they were surprised to learn that some of the things they were saying wrong—words that could destroy instead of build—were usually obvious to them, once they thought about it.

Those words or remarks to their children that were clearly negative, did not need a *new* set of words to replace them. It simply wasn't necessary to say them in the first place!

THERE ARE SOME THINGS WE SIMPLY SHOULDN'T SAY

How do you replace the comments that tell a young person he is "stupid," "lazy," or a "slow learner" with something positive? In most cases you don't have to. It usually isn't necessary to make a comment like that in the first place. You don't need a more positive way to tell a child he is clumsy or that you can't teach him anything.

Once we understand how the mind accepts the programming we receive from others, and how it acts on that programming as if it were true, how sensible can it be to go on saying things to young people that could clearly program them in the wrong way?

Certainly we are better custodians of our children's minds than to tell them *anything* that would create a picture of self-doubt, inability, or the fear of inadequacy in those minds. Would you want to hear that you are foolish, floundering, or inadequate? I certainly would not.

The children in our lives may not excel at everything they attempt, but most of them are better, more capable, than they are sometimes given credit for. They may not always be everything we would have hoped they would be, but there is not one of them who does not deserve the chance to be the best that he or she can be.

Why would we ever let any of our words to them

hold them back? Do we really want our children to be happy, delightful, energetic, enthusiastic, achieving, self-fulfilled, self-standing individuals? Of course we do. Do we want, in our hearts, to give them every chance, every positive self-belief, every moment of healthy, positive self-esteem, and every winning attitude that we can possibly deliver to them? We want that for them, and more.

Most of us have heard, years ago, that children become *most* what they *learn* most. We have all experienced how much criticism destroys and, in each of us, how much encouragement builds. And yet we forget sometimes what our own words, even without thinking about them, can do.

Why is it that we sometimes say exactly those things that we would never want someone to say to us? If you think about it, there is no reason to say, ever again, words like, "Let me do that for you, you'll never get it right," "You're just not cut out for that," "Can't you understand anything?" "You're not so special," "You don't know anything."

Those words need no replacement. We don't have to try to find some appropriate comment to make in their place. They need never be said at all.

Most of us would be amazed to find how many times a simple smile and a nod of understanding will say *everything* that is needed.

It is not necessary to learn how to replace words such as, "Jimmy, you'll never be as smart as your sister Sharon is in school," with something that is clearly the opposite, but clearly untrue. That would sound like nothing more than a fabrication and a false pat on the back.

Ask yourself, "What am I actually trying to say, what am I really trying to communicate? Am I trying to tell Jimmy that I think he's not smart? Or am I just trying to let him know that I am disappointed with his report card and I wish he could get good grades like his sister does?"

Then ask yourself, "What *could* I communicate if I really wanted to make the very *best* of this situation?"

WHEN IN DOUBT, DON'T SAY IT

Undoubtedly what you *really* want is the best for Jimmy. Convincing him that he doesn't measure up to someone else cannot possibly help him believe in himself. While your original words may have sprung from the disappointment you felt, the end result is that you communicate *exactly the opposite* of your best intentions.

When in doubt, *don't say it*!

That doesn't mean you should hold yourself back from expressing yourself or telling your child what you think. But think *first* of the real effect that your words will have—not just for the moment but in the pictures that your words create, the pictures your young person will carry with him for *years* to come.

If you find yourself saying something that communicates a picture of failure or self-doubt for that young person, stop yourself! Think for a moment. Ask yourself what you are really trying to say and what your *best* intentions are. And then say something that gets *those* intentions across—instead of defeating them.

What makes us say what we should not say? Sometimes it is frustration. Sometimes it is not knowing *what* to say. Sometimes it is habit. Sometimes it is simply that we were never taught what consequences our words could create. And sometimes, unfortunately, we say things we should not say because we are angry.

THE HARMFUL WORDS THAT ARE SPOKEN IN ANGER

The greatest creator of *"I ought to say the right thing, but I say the worst thing instead"* is, all too often, anger.

106

Most of us surprise even ourselves at times with the kinds of things we hear ourselves saying when we're upset.

And it is precisely when we are trying to set a child *straight* that we create some of the single *strongest* negative programs in the words we say to him.

When we get angry at a child or young person, we will often describe him, to himself, as *being* exactly the opposite of the way we would most like him to be. When we're angry, some of our words may describe how we feel about the youngster—*at the moment.* ("You're worthless!" "How stupid can you get?" "Don't you have *any* sense at all?") But do our words describe the internal image that we're really trying to give that child?

Because we say those words in anger, we usually give them a lot of energy. And words that are laced with strong emotional energy create strong emotional imprints—chemically and electrically—in the mind of the person we are talking to. That is a normal process of the subconscious mind:

The greater the emotion, the stronger the program.

When we are upset, some important mental chemicals get stirred up—and soon, so will our child's mental chemicals get stirred up.

The result of that chemistry is that we are telling the child some of the worst possible things about himself at precisely the time when the chemistry of his brain is so active that his imprinting will be strongest.

We give him, at that moment, an instant, powerful, *electrically and chemically* charged, mentally imprinted program that will become one of the *strongest* new programs in his subconscious mind.

PROGRAMS WE WOULD RATHER NOT CREATE

Few of the things we say in anger can be adequately taken back later, during a calmer, more caring moment. Once in place, the programs we deliver in anger usually stick. I have met adults who still struggle with things that were said to them in anger when they were small children.

It made little difference if the words were said in anger and not necessarily *true*. The messages they received, long ago, stayed with them. And those programs repeated and strengthened themselves in the self-talk of their own minds, playing out the wrong stories of "self." They repeat themselves like an endless videotape of the worst pictures of themselves, playing over and over again in their subconscious minds.

Some of those people have tried to live with those words, unsuccessfully, every day that followed, for the rest of their lives.

We do not usually say the wrong things in anger because we honestly believe them to be true. Nor do we usually believe that what we say in a moment of anger will *help*. We just say it because we're angry. Even though we know we shouldn't.

Angry, negative criticism, is one of the *least* effective ways to stop bad behavior in a child that we have ever found. In fact, it is the programs of criticism that we deliver in anger that are, in many instances, one of the leading *contributors* to bad behavior.

If you were able, at this moment, to remove every single *negative* program that was given to you by someone else during the first eighteen years of your life, it would be as though a great weight that you have carried with you for years were suddenly removed from you. You would notice the *difference* in yourself for the rest of your life.

When someone uses the wrong words at the wrong time, especially when those words are said or shouted in anger, even when the adult who is using them knows better, then the problem is not just the *child*—the problem is also the *adult*.

WHAT SEEMS HARMLESS
MAY NOT BE

Not all of the wrong kind of criticism is said in anger, of course. There is the kind of criticism that is handed out by even the calmest, most levelheaded of adults. And it is this kind of cool-headed, but often unknowing, negative programming that is the easiest to correct.

How? Stop doing it. Even if it has been merely an unconscious or occasional habit in the past, there is no reason, ever again, to say something to a young person (or anyone else for that matter) that could hurt them or cause them to see themselves as less than they could be.

What about those expressions or comments that on the *surface* appear to be neither positive nor negative, yet whose unconscious implication paints a negative picture for the child or young person? Some of these unrecognized parenting statements are among the most innocently given programs. There is no intentional affront, but the child's subconscious picks one up anyway.

This form of Parent-Talk is more subtle—it is harder to spot. But be on the lookout for it. One of my favorite examples of these hidden culprits of unconscious programmers is the statement, "You're just like your mother (or father, or brother, or sister, etc.)"—a comment that is usually told to a child only when he has done something wrong.

The underlying implication of the comment is that certain of the traits that, for example, both father and son have in common are bad. That communicates to the child a lot more than simply implying that he has just done something wrong—and the father has the same bad habit. It says to the child's subconscious mind that he has a basic flaw that he cannot change.

Another example, perhaps the most widely misused borderline program of the same kind, is the question, "Are you sure?" Or stated in other ways, the same question becomes, "Are you sure about that?" "What makes you so sure?" "I'm not so sure about that," or "How can you be so sure?"

The subconscious mind has no trouble interpreting that one. Read as: *"I question your judgment," "I don't trust you completely," "You don't know what you're talking about," "You'd better question what you think,"* or *"In this case I would recommend doubt."*

Children are already very often unsure of themselves —how can they be otherwise? They have a lot to learn and they sometimes know very little about a new situation they find themselves in. Why would we ever want to *add* to their self-doubt?

A BOY WHO WAS LOSING WHAT
LITTLE HE HAD

I once overheard a man talking to a boy, between twelve and fourteen years old, who was in a radio parts store buying some small parts for an electronics project. Each time the boy selected a resistor or a rectifier or a capacitor or a length of wire, the older man he was with questioned him. "Are you sure that's the right capacitance? Have you checked the schematic? Is that the right kind of wire? Are you sure you got enough of those? Shouldn't you get an extra one of those in case you make a mistake? Are you sure that's the right value of resistor? Are you sure that will work?"

I probably would not have noticed the two of them if the man had asked, "Are you sure . . . ?" only a time or two. But he continued to question the boy *in the same way* for fifteen or twenty minutes! By the time the boy took the parts he had finally selected to the checkout clerk, there was no doubt he was completely *unsure* and confused.

Several times he had made a well-chosen selection, only to put it back, pick it up again, and then finally change his mind, after the older man had completely undermined his sense of being able to make a simple decision for himself.

I learned later from the store manager that the young boy was an orphan, living in a foster care center and the older man was a volunteer parent, "helping" the boy out with one of the projects that he was working on at the center. None of us has to guess how much help the boy received.

If the "Are you sure . . . ?" message is received often enough, regardless of the circumstance, it can do nothing but instill self-doubt and destroy self-confidence. Even as adults we are not always *sure*. But as adults, we are at least given the right to be wrong—and learn from the mistake.

Testing our own ideas gives us the opportunity to measure our own feelings and to begin to recognize what a right choice feels like.

A child whose choice is questioned too often, or at inappropriate times, fails to learn what right choices feel like. And children who have grown up with frequent questioning of their choices usually live out a life plagued with indecision and self-doubt. And indecision and self-doubt lead to poor choices, false starts, low confidence, missed opportunities, poor organizational skills, and constant erosion of self-esteem.

All of that from words? Yes. All of that from words that were *unnecessary in the first place.*

WORDS THAT CREATE PROBLEMS INSTEAD OF SOLUTIONS

There are many examples of questionable Parent-Talk that are even less obvious. Do we really build a child's sense of self when we say something like, "You always insist on wearing that," "What do you see in him (or her) anyway?" "I know you're not telling me everything," "One day you'll be sorry," or "If only you knew."

The problem with each of these subtle comments is that they suggest a problem, but not one of them does *anything* to help fix the problem. And what we are saying out loud often delivers something to that person's subconscious that, if we thought about it, we would never want to say:

"I don't respect your judgment in your choice of the clothes you wear," "You are not able to choose the right friend (or mate)," "You're dishonest because you are hiding something from me," "Bad things are going to happen in your life," or "You are incapable of recognizing the realities of life."

Some of what we say in those instances may be true—at least to our way of looking at it, at the moment—but do we really want to convince the young person that what we are implying is intrinsically true of him?

It may be that the young person in question could use some help or advice, but what he hears, instead, is a reaffirmation of his *inability* to think or act in some way that we would like him to.

Does it do any good? Instead of doing any good for the young person, there is a good chance that it will only do the opposite.

NEVER SAY NEVER—IN THE NEGATIVE

Be careful of the use of the words *never* and *always* when they're used in a *negative* predictive way.

"You'll *never* get it right," "You *never* listen to me," "I'll *never* understand you," "I *always* have to tell you twice," "You *always* put your homework off till the last minute" may sound like some of the most common comments parents say. They are also some of the least effective (and sometimes most destructive) programs we could ever give.

The words *never* and *always* have an absoluteness about them—as though that is the way it is and it will never change. I, for one, would *never* like to hear the words "You'll *never* get it right" ever again. I would rather *always* be told, "You *always* get it right." I may never always get it right, but I would *always* know that I could.

MAKE SURE YOU'RE SPEAKING FOR YOURSELF

Anything we say to anyone, about anything, is affected by our *own* past programming. If you have said things to your children in the past that it is now obvious were the wrong things to say—and may have given them some wrong programs—don't be too hard on yourself.

Few of us were taught early enough the effects that our own words could have. And meanwhile, you and I were being programmed with words from others. *Their* programs to *us* set up a pattern for our subconscious minds to follow. Some of our files got filled with less than the best of programs.

So we talk to our kids in a way that seems most natural to us. Since our speech and behavior are the results of *our* own internal programs, we pass some of that same kind of programming along to them.

Once we become aware of it, however, that should begin to change. Many of the parenting programs we received may have been excellent. But if, along the way, we picked up some habits and ideas that are not right for us, it only makes sense to change them. If we want to talk to our kids today in the best way possible, we may have to make some changes in our own Self-Talk and fix a few programs of our own.

Let's say that as of this moment you make the decision to teach yourself to be so aware of everything you say to your child that you will never again say anything that will create vague, negative, or harmful programs. Instead, whenever possible, you will say those things that will help create healthy programs.

Let's also say that you will practice doing this *consciously*—at least during the time that you are getting started—during the next few weeks. Your intention is to make this new parenting style so natural and so automatic that in time you will do it without having to be consciously aware of working at it.

If our old programming is dictating behaviors in ourselves that cause us to say the *wrong* things to our kids, then we also have to work on our *own* programming. If you would like to replace some of the earlier programs in your own files with programs about yourself that work better for you, you may want to use some of the Self-Talk suggestions that are discussed in Chapter 19 to help you get started.

But even without a new set of programs for ourselves, any of us who choose to can make the decision to stop using words and comments that never build, but instead question or take something away.

Getting rid of the wrong kinds of words isn't difficult. It just takes thought. Never again saying something that would work against your child doesn't ask you to do the impossible. It just asks you to do something that you're probably good at already: It just asks you to care.

Chapter 11

What *Should* You Say?

There are times when something we have typically said in the past *should* be replaced—with something better. Some old Parent-Talk may need to have some new, more effective Parent-Talk to take its place.

But when parents or teachers begin to practice changing what they say, they are sometimes at a loss for a better set of programs—new, more positive comments to use in place of the old negative statements.

I am often asked by parents, "How can I tell Kenny he's terrific when he *isn't*? Why should I tell Suzie she is neat and organized, when her room is never less than a total mess? How can I tell Craig he has a good attitude when he's down in the mouth about everything? How can I tell Mike he's just as athletic as his brother, when his brother excels at every sport he tries out for, and Mike doesn't?"

After all, we do want to tell them the *truth* about themselves, don't we?

Or what about those times when we have no choice but to mete out punishment of one kind or another? How can you help a young person feel good about himself or herself when even the simple act of punishment or the simple words of reprimand that we are obligated to deliver are proof positive that, at least in some respect, he or she is not doing so well?

What *should* we say? What can we say, instead of those dozens or hundreds of things we might have said in the past and gotten *used* to saying, that will create a better program for the child—and still be *true*?

BEGIN BY TELLING THEM ABOUT THE FILES IN THEIR MINDS

The parents who take the time to explain the "mental filing cabinets" and at least a simplified picture of the programming process of the human brain, to their children, have an easier time with this one.

Once the child understands what positive programming is and how the files work, he will begin to understand at least something about why you say certain things to him in a certain way.

If your son or daughter is old enough to understand how the process works, it can help to explain about those filing cabinets in his or her mind.

Even children who are quite young seem to be able to grasp the picture of papers with words on them placed in files and stuffed into the drawers of filing cabinets in a giant room that is *full* of files.

Older kids have no problem understanding at all. Kids today have grown up with computers and the word "program," and they grasp the concepts of computer information storage and retrieval sometimes more quickly than do their parents.

When parents explain to their children how the filing cabinets of the mind work and that what they put into those files will have an effect on their future, those parents are giving their children an important insight into their relationship.

Those children have a better chance of understanding that what their parents do and say is the result of love, caring, belief, support, guidance, and respect—exactly the gifts that the child needs most.

When the child understands even a little about the process, he begins to *listen* differently. Now when the parent says to the child, "Laura, your room is a mess, *but I know that's not really like you—you're good at keeping it clean, too*," Laura, even if she's no more than five or six years old, begins to understand. Describing this process to a young person does not mean that you should have a deep intellectual discussion with him or her about the complexities of the human brain. A few simple illustrations will usually do the trick.

GETTING STARTED WITH A NEW WAY TO SAY IT

I would certainly encourage you to take the time to explain to your child some of what we know about "how we grow—in our *minds*."

But even if you have not yet taught your child the basics of how what we are told and what we say to ourselves will affect nearly everything about us, you can still change much of what you say to him, and it will still have a positive effect—even if he doesn't yet understand how it works.

Opportunities to change what we say to our kids come up daily. And you soon learn to make the change in what you say and naturally deal with the new style of speaking to them. In time, making minor changes in what you say to them happens almost unconsciously.

Words such as, *"Don't bother me now, can't you see I'm busy?"* become, *"I'd really like you to tell me about that. I'm busy right now, but let's talk about it just as soon as I'm through."*

When you are talking to a child who has overstepped his boundaries and broken the rules, statements such as, *"Who do you think you are, anyway?"* can be changed to put better pictures of self-identity into his mental file folders.

It's not difficult to change statements like those into healthier statements such as, *"I happen to think you're pretty special, but we still have to follow the rules."* With practice, it is possible to say something productive, even when you are *upset* with the child.

"Can't you do **anything** right?" is better stated, *"There are a lot of things you're very good at. In time I think you'll have **this** one mastered, too."* A statement such as, *"You can try it, but I don't think it's going to work,"* can become, *"I'm proud of you for trying it, and I believe in you. I know that you'll do the best that you can."*

Does making that change expect too much of the child or ignore the facts? No it doesn't. It simply puts the most positive possible construction on the situation at hand.

Clearly counterproductive statements like, *"Haven't I taught you anything?"* could fall into that category of statements we discussed in the previous chapter—statements that could be dropped entirely.

But if you find yourself in a situation where you feel you *have* to say *something,* try changing it to, *"It's really important to me to help you learn everything that I can. And by the way, that's because **you're** important to me."* Or why not say, *"I'd like to show you again how that works,"* or *"I'd like to explain that again,"* or *"Doesn't it feel great when you figure it out and it really works for you?"*

119

Saying something such as, *"Why should I give you an-other chance?"* instills nothing but self-doubt and a sense of worthlessness in the mind of a child. It is much better to say, *"Do you know why I'm going to give you another chance? Because I believe in you!"* That is a complete switch in the internal program you just gave your youngster—and a potential switch in the results next time around.

FINDING THE RIGHT WORDS

There are times when you may have to search a bit to find something particularly productive to say about the young person to help him see a better picture of himself, especially when he has just done something wrong or failed badly. It doesn't do much good to dwell on the mistake or the problem.

And the long-term result will be improved if, instead, you replace a "replay of the disaster" with a different picture that *predicts* success! Proof to his or her young mind that he or she *does* have value, after all—in spite of the mistake—will either be offered or withheld, by the words you choose at the moment.

I remember the time, years ago, when I was learning to drive. My father decided that a tractor he owned would be the safest vehicle for me to learn on. Within sixty seconds of the moment I popped the clutch and lurched forward, I ran headlong into a small tree. I wasn't hurt, neither was the tree, and neither was the tractor, but we certainly could have been.

I remember that my fear of hitting the tree was nothing compared with my fear of what my father would say next. But instead, my father came running up, looked at me, looked at the tree, smiled, and said, "Well, *you almost missed it!*"

Not only was he smart enough to go for the positive, but in that one small statement, instead of making me feel like I was clumsy or stupid (which is how I had felt only a moment earlier), he got me to believe that I *could* do it right.

I have wondered since that time about some of the words that fathers and mothers, over the years, must surely have yelled at youngsters (before the years of driver-training classes at school). What must some of them have said when their son or daughter backed off the curb or turned an attempt at parallel parking into some strange way of maneuvering a car so that its tail end stuck out six feet into the middle of a busy lane of oncoming traffic?

Or what about those times when that first fender connected with that first tree or didn't quite make it through the garage door? I suspect that what some of those parents actually said could not be printed here. I give the parents who kept their cool, and said something nice, credit for having an early sense of Predictive Parenting.

PRAISE ALONE IS NOT THE ANSWER

We have been told that it works better to praise than to criticize. And that is true. But replacing criticism with praise is only a small part of Predictive Parenting.

It is not our intent to suddenly begin painting our children as wonderful beings that only moments ago stepped down from heaven. It is important to be practical, realistic, and honest. But how honest is it to say to a

121

teenage son or daughter, *"This is the last time I'm going to tell you," "Nothing I say makes any difference to you," "You don't care about anything!" "You're lucky to even be living here,"* or, *"All you know how to do is cause problems"*?

It is certainly not realistic to tell even the smallest children such things as, *"When you grow up, you're going to be chubby, just like your Aunt Harriet,"* or *"You'll never be an artist—you don't have the talent for it," "I've tried everything to get you to stop wetting the bed, and nothing works," "You're just a little chatterbox,"* or *"You just can't pay attention, can you?"*

When we say these things, is what we say really the *truth* or is it only a projection of our own disbelief and doubt, brought on by the moment, by something our child has said or done?

At the moment it may *appear* to be true—but does what we are saying describe an attitude or a particular behavior? Is the child really the way we are describing him or her to be? Often the child inside may be nothing at all like the description we are repeating to him.

We have all heard parents give their children self-descriptions that sound like, *"You can't sit still for a minute," "Your hair is just impossible—there's absolutely nothing that can be done with it,"* or something as potentially destructive as, *"You're just a natural-born liar."* To the real child *inside,* those words are not only untrue—they are terribly unfair.

HOW DID IT MAKE YOU FEEL?

Think back to your own childhood. How did you feel when someone told you that you were failing, dishonest, impossible, difficult, incapable, slow, talked too much, wouldn't pay attention, were disorganized, or anything else that told you that *that* was how some adult *believed* you to be?

It may be true that among the particular children in question in the earlier examples the child may not have been able to stop wetting the bed, a girl's hair is constantly in tangles, a young boy has gotten caught in yet another lie, or a child's school papers disclose the obvious fact that his crayons somehow find it difficult to stay in the lines.

But what *should* you say? Replace the old words with words that build instead of words that create defeat. Give them words that find the good in them instead of giving them words that prove to them that their failure is a true picture of "the way they *are*."

If you were one of those children, in the same circumstance, what would you want someone to say to you? Would you want to be convinced that you were failing or would you like to know that even your failures are part of learning—and that *someone* believes that you can rise above them?

I think that most of us would choose to have someone guide us and help us, and above all, see us as being capable of overcoming our short-term inadequacies and replacing them with more of our true, more successful selves.

We're not perfect. And with enough of our own self-esteem working for us, neither would we want anyone else to expect us to be. But I have never met a single individual who did not want to be given a chance to feel good about himself. A child doesn't have to be very old for us to begin to see that look in his or her eyes that says, "Did I do all right? Am *I* all right?"

THE FEAR OF DISAPPROVAL

Watch your child the next time he stumbles and falls. What does he do first? *He looks to see who saw him fall.* Watch a child recite the words of a poem or something he is supposed to memorize for school. When he makes a mistake, what will he almost always do first? He will look up, very quickly, at the listener, and then his eyes will dart down for a brief instant, before he begins again.

In that short time, what is he doing? He is recognizing his mistake, checking for approval or disapproval, searching for what he should have said, and criticizing himself internally for doing something wrong.

If you watch closely, you will also see the signs of frustration and self-doubt—a slight movement of his head, much as he would if he were unconsciously shaking his head and telling himself no. All of us have been there. We know the feeling.

At that moment he knows he didn't do it right—and all too frequently, he is about to be told, by one of us, that his worst fear is true: We disapprove. That same scenario is played out thousands of times in different situations in a child's young life.

It is played out at report-card time, at Little League ball games, at the dinner table, in public when manners are momentarily misplaced, in the classroom, with friends, when doing something new, when doing chores, when trying to tell us something he or she did that day, when almost any mistake is made or when that child does something wrong, behaves badly, or when he or she is expected to do something and fails to do it right.

Of course, we can say that's how we learn. And that's true—that *is* how we learn a lot of what ends up getting programmed into us. That's how we learn to do better, learn more, grow up, and act right. We learn who we are,

124

what we can do, how far we should reach, and what we should expect of ourselves.

But learning to do things "right" is only a *part* of what we learn. In the process we learn about *ourselves.* Along with learning the "rules" growing up, we also begin to accept a growing composite picture of ourselves that those thousands of minor experiences help create.

It is in that natural learning process that we first also learn to believe what we *cannot* achieve, how far we should *not* reach, what we do wrong—instead of right—and what *not* to expect of ourselves.

It is while we are learning the rules to follow that we also learn the programs that will end up holding us back. *It is during those incredibly important growing years that we learn to accept our imagined limitations and to lose sight of the potential that we were born with.*

Some of those programs will (unless we finally learn to change them for ourselves later), literally guide our destinies; they are childhood programs that will direct us for the rest of our lives. And unfortunately, as we have learned, many of them are the *wrong* programs.

You cannot overestimate the value of the words you use when you have the opportunity to parent or to teach. There will be times—perhaps many of them—when the old words of parenting—those things you might have said in the past—are clearly no longer the right words to use.

PICTURES OF THE BEST PERSPECTIVE

Learn to modify the old words. Replace them with pictures that give your child the best possible perspective of himself. Work at it if you have to; think about what you say, listen to your thoughts, challenge yourself to deliver the best possible word pictures you can come up with.

It doesn't take any more time to say, *"Your coloring looks fun,"* or *"Your coloring is pretty,"* or *"You could be an artist someday—in fact, you already are an artist—the more you learn the better you'll get!"* When a child tells a lie, try saying, *"The truth is really more fun than a lie. Anyone can tell a lie. But you're good at the truth. I believe in you, deep down inside, and so do you."*

The parent in the earlier example who told her daughter that nothing was working to help her stop wetting the bed may want to try a different approach: *"It's fun to feel warm and dry and cozy at night. Keep smiling, tonight just could be the night!"* What a different self-picture those words begin to create.

In none of those examples did we create an untruth or a false expectation. Instead, we recognized a new truth, and added the energy of sincere and enthusiastic expectancy and belief. Said in the right way, each of those statements becomes a gift from the parent to the child.

Imagine tagging all of the parenting words you use, that gave your child belief and encouragement, with a bright yellow "sunburst," in the form of a small adhesive label glued to the corner of each file that held those words in the files in your child's mind.

If you could do that, and if you visited your child's mental filing room and walked through it and opened all of the filing cabinets, how many sunbursts would you see in the files that your child has stored in that room?

If each time a negative or potentially misguiding statement was made to your child, you pasted a small gray "rain cloud" sticker to the corner of that file, how many dark stickers would you find on the corners of those files?

Looking at childhood conditioning at its most primary level, the future success, happiness, and self-actualization of your child—years from now, as an adult—will have a direct relationship to the number of bright sunbursts or dark clouds that paint the files in that child's mind.

That is a simplified look at conditioning, of course. We know that the relationship between what we say to our kids and the effects our words will have in their lives is more complex than that.

In fact, the relationship between our programming and the results of that programming is part of an astoundingly complex electrochemical mechanism that includes billions of intricate circuits and tens of billions of messages that flash incessantly along electrical and chemical pathways in the brain.

Those pathways guide the message to their proper destinations, separating and sorting, cataloging and filing, driving and directing them through the most complex biological and chemical information storage and retrieval mechanism that mankind has ever witnessed or explored—the brain, the mind; the mechanism that controls the destiny of each human being.

But the link is clear; the tie is irrefutable. The direct link between the programs we receive and the pictures of ourselves that we end up carrying around with us is now known. Can changes in the words we use when we talk to our kids have that much importance?

They can and they do.

Each time we add one of those seemingly insignificant statements of positive direction to our child's bank of internal programs, we add positive *energy* to that child's mind.

Our words—and the thoughts our words create in our child's mind—trigger powerful chemicals in the brain that imprint circuits, store the information we give them, and offer that child an exciting new wealth of consciously programmed alternatives. Children are not robots—far from it. But they are, in a very natural way, programmed—strongly and often indelibly—by the words we choose when we talk to them.

When in doubt, take the time to think about what you

127

really mean and say it. That is the basis of all good communication. There is no reason to offer our children anything less.

A LITTLE AWARENESS AND A LOT OF COMMON SENSE

I am not suggesting that we should have to live our parenting lives worried about the implication of every word we say. But I am suggesting an overall awareness of our words—and that we use common sense. As parents and teachers, we begin to win and we begin to help our kids win, when we decide to change some of what we have said to our kids in the past.

Earlier we discussed the possible changes in your life that you could create just by getting rid of every one of the unnecessary negative programs that you received in the first eighteen years of your life. If you were also able to replace each of those previous negative programs with a powerful *new* positive program, you would achieve for yourself what most of us are looking for in our own lives—and what we now have the chance to give to our children.

Chapter 12

The Messages They Need to Hear

Let's take a closer look at some of the words of parenting and find out if what we say to our children really gives their minds the pictures they need, *pictures to pattern their lives on.*

What are the words they really need to hear, to create the best pictures of themselves in the subconscious "identity centers" of their minds?

When we talk to our kids, what do the words we use really say to them? What pictures do we paint for them in their minds, and what pictures (of themselves) would give them the best chance for a "successful" life?

For our examples, we'll select a few of the statements we saw earlier, statements that some parents have said to their kids. In each example we'll ask two important questions:

1. *What do our words* really *mean to the child's unconscious picture of himself?*

2. *What are the messages that our children really need to hear?*

What we say when we talk to our kids is always interpreted, unconsciously, in our child's mind. What we hear ourselves saying out loud may sound nothing at all like the real messages we are unknowingly giving to our child's subconscious.

For example, when we say to a child the words *"When will you ever learn?"* what we think we are saying and what our child's subconscious mind picks up may be two different messages entirely!

When we say, "When will you ever learn?" (which is usually said to a child when he has done something wrong—*again*), we are trying to express our frustration with a mistake the child has repeated. We'd like him to learn that what he did was "wrong" so he won't make the same mistake again.

To us the question "When will you ever learn?" is a simple one. It doesn't sound like it could give our child a negative program about himself—and yet, that is exactly what it does.

What the child hears (unconsciously) could be a far stronger message than we had intended to give. To the child, the words can all too easily be translated to read *"You are probably going to make the same mistake again," "You will never learn," "You're not very good at following rules,"* or *"I don't have faith in you."*

Did we really intend to imply any of these things? No, we didn't. But the subconscious mind of the child doesn't know that. It is designed to take whatever input it is given, find the files that have already stored information that is similar, and add one more file entry to that file.

Recognizing that, in this example it would be more valuable to the child's picture of his own "learning ability" to put our words a different way.

If we are aware that what we would really like to be doing is giving that child something positive about his learning skills—something he can use to grow on instead of something that creates a picture of doubt about himself in his mind—it would be more worthwhile to say something else entirely.

In this instance, it might be a good idea to say, *"I know you're working at doing better, and I think you're going to get it right!"*

Then state your piece—reset the rules, discuss the problem, or get across whatever message you really want to give. But by starting your first comments off on the right foot, you not only give your comments a better chance of being listened to, but you have also reinforced a positive program in the child's mind instead of making a *negative* program stronger.

WHAT IS THE MESSAGE THEY NEED TO HEAR?

There are countless examples of almost unnoticed statements that we make to children. Some of those statements build belief and self-worth in the child—and help us deal with the situation effectively. Some of them do not.

In the following examples we'll look at a few of the kinds of statements that work against our children—instead of for them. You may not say any of these specific things when you talk to your kids, but you can use the same analysis with anything you say.

EXAMPLE #1

Statement: *"I wish I could believe you."*

What It Says (to the child's mind):
"I don't believe you." "You don't tell the truth." "You say things that can't be trusted." "You're not an honest

person." "Even if you are telling the truth this time, I can't accept it."

The Real Message He or She Needs to Hear:
"I may not believe what you just said, but I know you are an honest person." "You're good at telling the truth." "I trust you a lot." "Let's talk about this. I trust you and I want to help you be the honest person that you are."

Let's look at another example. In this example the child may have done something as simple as leaving his homework at school, or perhaps he didn't put dishwashing detergent in the dishwasher, played with friends instead of coming right home after school as he was told, left a bicycle in the middle of the driveway, tracked mud into the house, played in his new jeans and got holes in the knees, set a glass of milk too close to the edge of the table and knocked it off, or stayed out too late without calling home. In any of these cases, parents might tell him or her, "You just don't *think!*"

EXAMPLE #2

Statement: *"You just don't think!"*

What It Says to the Child:
"You are inconsiderate." "You don't care enough to do the right thing." "You *don't* think, therefore you may not be *capable* of thinking." "I fully expect you to do the same thing again." "You are a person who *never* thinks about the consequences of what you do." "You do not take personal responsibility for yourself." "Even if you thought you were thinking, it's clear that your best is not good enough."

Imagine sending those "directives" to a child's control center and saying, "This is *who* you are and *how* you are.

This is the picture of you that you should accept and act out."

Unless he receives enough positive-programming messages to the contrary, he *will* attempt to act out the negative programs.

The Real Message He or She Needs to Hear:
"You have a good *mind* and you really *think* well!" "You may have made a mistake by not thinking, but that doesn't mean you are not good at thinking things out—you *are* good at thinking, and you do it often." "You have a good sense of responsibility." "You always figure out what will happen because of what you do." "I *like* the way you think."

EXAMPLE #3

Statement: *"All you ever do is argue."*

What It Says to the Child:
"You don't really know how to communicate." "You do not have the ability to listen and understand." "You do not value someone else's point of view." "I do not value your point of view when it disagrees with mine." "You do not care about others." "Don't think for yourself—your opinion doesn't count." "When you express yourself, you always create a problem."

Those unconscious statements to that child's mind may be a true reflection of the way the child is acting at the moment—but *are they* a true reflection of the directions and pictures we would like the child to place in the information filing center in his or her mind? The image we would *like* to cement in place is probably something far different:

The Real Message He or She Needs to Hear:
"I really like talking with you." "You listen to other

people when they talk." "I respect your opinions." "You are learning to think for yourself—and you have a lot of good ideas." "You make your point and you leave it at that." "You express yourself well."

When messages like those are given to a child's subconscious mind, what does it hear? To find out, take those same words, rephrase them, and look at the self-directions a child's subconscious mind has available to it to act on—when it is given the right input to work with in the first place. To a child's subconscious mind, those new words would say:

"People really like talking to me. I listen when other people talk. Other people respect my opinions. I am learning to think for myself and I have a lot of good ideas. I make my point and I leave it at that. I express myself well."

That attitude is a sign of healthy self-esteem. And it is typical of *exactly* the kind of internal attitude that most of us would like to see in our children. In the examples that follow, try the same thing. Take the words that children "need to hear" and turn them around in the same way. In every case they are the words of positive self-direction and strong self-esteem.

EXAMPLE #4

Statement: *"I just don't think you're cut out for that."*

A parenting statement of this kind is often said when a child attempts to do something new—and doesn't do it too well, or when a young person talks about a goal that he or she is thinking about pursuing.

Whether it is planting a row of flowers behind the house, trying out for cheerleading, or attempting a project for science class, sometimes, before they have even had a chance to *disqualify* the idea on their own or try the idea out long enough to test the possibility, we insert our own doubts into their internal belief system.

What It Says to the Child:
"You aren't capable." "You don't have the talent for that." "You won't like it even if you do it." "You do not have the ability to develop the skill." "Your future is already preset for you." "Don't try to build strengths when you don't have them in you." "I'd like you to live *my* way." "Some people could succeed at that but you won't." "Why even try?"

The Real Message He or She Needs to Hear:
"You are incredibly capable!" "If you put your mind to it, you can do it." "I really admire you for making good choices." "If that's what you want to do, I'm behind you all the way." "I believe in you."

EXAMPLE #5

Statement: *"This is the last time I'm going to tell you."*

What It Says to the Child:
"I am not willing to be patient with you." "You're not worth the effort it takes to help you get it right." "You are a slow learner." "You don't do things right." "You need more instruction than you deserve." "You don't live up to my expectations of you." "You make it difficult for me to help you." "I find it hard to deal with you." "You never listen when I talk to you."

You may have to let your child know that you *aren't* going to continue to put up with a problem he's creating. But even when you do that, the message you send might just as well be one that offers direction for the child to behave in a more positive or beneficial way in the future.

The Real Message He or She Needs to Hear:
"Believe it or not, I *still* believe in you, and I'm still on

your side." "You are worth every effort it takes to help you get it right." "You are capable and you can do it." "You do *many* things well—and you can do this well too." "Sometimes I am impatient with you, but I sometimes forget that growing up takes time." "You always end up doing your best, and your best is very good."

EXAMPLE #6

Statement: *"You never finish anything on time."*

Statements like this can give *lifelong* misdirection to young minds. What they say to the child's sense of *self-*direction can create untold negative consequences for them throughout the rest of their lives.

If a child is told something like that often enough, his or her unknowing young mind *will* accept, program it in, and *believe* it!

The message that those simple words deliver to the receptive young mind of a child is a message that *none* of us would like to receive—and have to live out for the rest of our lives.

What It Says to the Child:

"You don't get things done." "You can't be counted on." "You are always late with everything you do." "You are not organized." "You don't have good work habits." "You put things off." "You don't have the ability to do what you need to do when you need to do it." "You will probably always be this way."

Imagine what that self-picture, firmly set in place in a young person's mind, would do to his or her future school assignments, personal responsibilities, job or career, and overall self-esteem.

Having an organized mind and a sense of "timeliness" is not an inborn trait. It is learned. It is a part of each person's *internal* development and self-picture. There are better programs or pictures that could be given:

The Real Message He or She Needs to Hear:
"You *really* know how to get things done." "The more you practice getting things done on time, the better things will work for you." "Let me help you learn to work at doing things when they need to be done." "Things work better for us when we do things on time." "You have a lot of ability to plan things so that everything fits." "You will always be one of those people who gets things done."

EXAMPLE #7

Statement: *"Now look what you've done!"*

The nature of *learning* demands that we make mistakes along the way. That is, after all, one of the ways we learn.

Whether a child or a young person has ruined a new dress or a pair of pants, broken a lamp, spilled watercolor paint on the carpet, broken the screen door, ruined the roast, or dented the fender on the car, few of them set out to do it.

With that fact in mind, it doesn't make a lot of sense to turn the problem of the moment into the kind of negative predictive programming that sets them up to see that "mistake" as a basic part of the internal picture they are creating of themselves.

What It Says to the Child:
"You always make mistakes." "Why should I trust you to do things right?" "Once again, you have done something wrong. . . . I can only assume that you will continue to do things wrong." "I do not approve of you." "You can't do anything right." "I am losing patience

with your mistakes." "You *constantly* do things wrong." "You are supposed to be better than you are." "You are judged by the mistakes you make."

Think about a time when you were criticized for something you did when you were young. If you felt bad or embarrassed at the time, did you hear only the few words that were said to you, or did your own feelings add *more* of the same kinds of words?

For most of us, the embarrassment, frustration, and even *self*-criticism that *we* add to the criticism we received from someone else make us feel even worse!

When a youngster makes a mistake, will the first impressions his or her mind picks up be those of acceptance or those of disapproval? Few kids ever *try* to make mistakes. But when they do, what is said to them *next* will send messages to their minds that go far beyond the words they hear.

Fortunately, the same is true of the words children hear that give them support and acceptance. Instead of saying something like, "Now look what you've done!" try a different approach.

The Real Message He or She Needs to Hear:
"It's okay, you're all right. You didn't do anything wrong." "That's how we learn!" "I know you didn't mean to do that." "I still like you!" "Are *you* okay?" "I see you've just learned something that doesn't work." "You're a good kid." "I've done the same thing myself." "Sometimes these things happen to the nicest people." "That's okay, next time you'll do better." "I love you anyway."

If you already say something like that, give yourself a gold star. That's Predictive Parenting in one of its most *worthwhile* forms.

EXAMPLE #8

Statement: *"Your room is always a mess"*

This is one of my favorite examples of bad programming. One mother told me that if I could do nothing more than teach parents how to help their kids keep their rooms straightened up, it would be worth a million dollars.

She might have been a bit extravagant in her claims, but she was right about how difficult something as basic as "personal organization" can be for kids in a lot of homes.

I won't tell you that a few words will suddenly change your children's bedrooms into the rooms we see in model homes, but I will tell you that what you say to them—in *spite of* what you may have come to believe—does make a difference.

Look at what the repeated message "Your room is always a mess" actually tells our children about their rooms—and about *themselves:*

What It Says to the Child:

"You are not capable of keeping your room clean (or neat)." "You are disorganized." "No matter what you do, you can always expect to have a messy room." "I fully expect and believe that the organization of your room will *never* get any better." "You do not have good organizational habits." "You like to live in a cluttered environment." "You do not know how to put things in their proper places." "The place you live is not important to you." "You do not take the time to be neat and orderly."

Imagine the consequences of *that* kind of programming in later life! What would it do to that future adult's home or that future adult's job? "Organizational skills" in almost any career or job are among the most important skills a person can master.

How well will a child ever be able to master those skills if he or she is taught to believe, *unconsciously,* that the *ability* to master those skills just isn't *there*?

The Real Message He or She Needs to Hear:
"You are organized and you have things under control." "You are learning to do a good job of keeping your room neat." "You've got a lot of good habits." "You have a good mind. You think clearly, and you organize your thoughts." "You take care of things that are important to you." "You take the time to do things right." "You take responsibility for yourself and for everything you do."

Sometimes parents say things to even very young children that would be much better said a different way. At the time a young child first hears these words, he or she may not even understand their implications. But kids are pretty good at figuring things out. In time they learn to understand the messages we are giving them.

I first heard the following comment at the home of friends I was visiting. I later heard the same words repeated to one of the children at a day care center by one of his "teachers." It is one of those simple remarks that crops up again and again in the lives of some children.

Imagine what a seemingly "harmless" few words, such as the following comment, repeated often enough might instill in the mind of even a three- or four-year-old child:

EXAMPLE #9

Statement: *"You're just a troublemaker."*

What It Says to the Child:
"Causing trouble gets you noticed." "Instead of making

my life happy and peaceful, you make things difficult."
"You will always cause problems—that's just the way
you are." "I *expect* you to be a troublemaker." "You're
good at causing trouble." "You are *different* from the
other children because of the trouble you make."

The Real Message He or She Needs to Hear:
"You are *not* a troublemaker." "I notice you because
you are *you,* not because you sometimes do things to
get my attention." "You *don't* cause problems." "You
really have fun getting along with the rest of the kids."
"It's okay to try new things, but it's not okay to make
things go wrong. Some kids do that, but you don't
have to."

It isn't hard to imagine that same child, ten or twelve
years later, if he has only learned to believe that he *is* a
"troublemaker," growing up being told more of the same.
By now he is an adolescent, and his old programming has
already convinced him that the next negative programming he receives about himself is also probably true:

EXAMPLE #10

Statement: *"You'll never amount to anything!"*

What It Says to the Young Person:
"You have no real value or worth." "You will never
become what you wanted to be." "I do not believe in
you." "You don't do anything right." "You have no
reason to respect who you are." "You are not as good as
others." "You are not capable of becoming an exceptional person." "You are a disappointment to me." "No
matter how hard you try, it still won't work." "I do not
accept you or believe in you." "You are not special."
"Life will always be difficult for you."

When a teenager hears words that undermine a self-belief that is already doubt-ridden and shaky, those words convince him that the negative things he has feared about himself are true.

What that same teenager needs to hear, inside, is not another self-portrait of incompetence. What he or she needs to hear, and what we would most like to give, is a message that builds hope and self-worth:

The Real Message He or She Needs to Hear:
"You are incredible!" "You have value and worth." "I like who you are!" "You are a special, important, unlimited human being." "I care about you and so do you." "You are more than I had ever known." "You can be trusted." "You take responsibility for yourself." "You make good decisions and good choices." "I value your judgment." "I may tell you that I want the best for you, but I also know that you want the best for yourself." "You are *unbelievably, incredibly* important."

I doubt that there is a teenager living today who would not like to hear—and believe—those words. I have never met *anyone* who would not like to hear them. The more we say those words, the more we *believe* in them when we talk to our kids, the more we make them true.

In an earlier example we took the words that a child's mind "needs to hear" and turned them around so that we could see the message of those positive statements—a message that the child's subconscious mind would hear and store.

In this case, with the right words, the message that the young person's subconscious mind hears would sound like this:

"I am incredible! I have worth and value. My mother (or father) likes who I am. I am a special, important, unlimited human being. I am cared

about and I care about myself. I am more than I had ever known. I can be trusted. I take responsibility for myself. I make good decisions and good choices. People value my judgment. Other people may tell me that they want the best for me, but I also want the best for myself. I am unbelievably, incredibly important."

What an exceptional sense of positive self that picture gives. I can't imagine any parent, at any time, *not* wanting his or her child to have *that* kind of picture of himself. It is an incredible portrait of a young person who is ready to live a life of value and worth.

WHAT IS THE "PICTURE" OF THEMSELVES THAT YOU REALLY WANT TO GIVE THEM?

There are many things that we say to our kids—no matter how positively we have been talking to them in the past—that we could change to give them one more moment of predictive encouragement.

For even one week or one month, do with your own parenting words what we just did in these few examples. Look at what you may have said before, ask yourself what it really says to the mind of your child, and decide whether or not it really says what you would like it to say.

If your words paint the pictures you want your child to hold of himself in his mind, keep using them. If they do not, ask yourself what better words you might say.

I have often thought that many kids have been hearing the wrong things. I know that as parents, we wanted them to hear the right things. We just didn't know what to say.

Chapter 13

The View from the Mind of a Child

Have you ever seen a father who is trying to help a youngster with his homework when, no matter how hard he tries, he can't get his point across? I know parents who swear they have *given up* helping with homework for good because of the frustration that goes along with it.

How many times do we as parents think that our message should be clear—when, to the child, our message is not clear at all? I have heard parents who were sitting at a nearby table at a restaurant repeat the same exact words of direction to a child, four or five times in a row, somehow expecting that repetition creates understanding. (It doesn't.)

During a Little League game I attended, I heard an angry father telling his teenage son to be more "responsible" and to act like a "grown-up." The father may not have known that his own view of "responsibility" and that of his son's were more than likely entirely different.

A YOUNG PERSON'S VIEW OF THE WORLD

A child's *view* of life is different from ours. As adults, most of us have a reasonable grasp of the events that go on in the world around us. We understand the meanings of most of the words we hear. Every word we use or hear already has a cluster of pictures and thought patterns attached to it based on our own past experiences.

Every thought we think is already tied to a stack of mental pictures and meanings that give us a broad spectrum from which to view life. Mental pictures—knowledge—give a form of "instant meaning" to almost every new word or experience that we encounter.

We have spent *years* getting our own filing cabinets filled up. Our mental programs are *full* of references that tell us what to think and how to feel about almost anything that happens in our lives. When a new situation comes up for us, if we haven't experienced the same situation in the past, we at least have some experience to relate that new experience to.

What we have come to believe and accept about nearly every detail of the world around us is already stored in the files of our experienced, adult minds. Our beliefs, attitudes, emotional responses, and behavior styles have already been programmed for us.

Because of the vast number of programs we have stored up, as adults, we tend to become somewhat set in our ways. You and I have learned to react and respond to things in certain ways just as our banks of programming files tell us to. Our child's mind attempts to do the same thing. It just doesn't have as much previously filed information to go on yet.

A good way to view the mind of a child or a young

145

person is to look at his or her mind from inside the mental room of filing cabinets that we looked at earlier. Are the files mostly full, or are they still mostly empty? Is there some information in every file—and what does that information say?

Because learning is a gradual process that moves us from birth to maturity and beyond, the emptier those filing cabinets are, the more influence we as parents potentially have. And along with that influence, the more responsibility we have to ensure that our children receive the right files—the knowledge and directions necessary to prepare them to become self-reliant adults.

If we don't recognize that difference, it is all too easy to expect a child or a young person to think as we think or to see life as we see it. To children, life is made up of *only what they already know*.

LIVING ON THE FORTY-SECOND FLOOR

I remember the story of a family who lived on the forty-second floor of a high-rise building on the lakefront in Chicago.

Each morning the two-year-old son kissed his father good-bye as his father stepped into the elevator, which was located just outside the door to their apartment. Each night the boy waited to jump into his father's arms as he stepped back off the same elevator.

It was only later, after the boy had learned to express himself clearly, that the family learned that for many months the little boy had thought his dad spent his entire day, every day, on the elevator.

AN OFFICE COMMUNICATOR—
WHO DOESN'T
COMMUNICATE AT HOME

Children have the right and need to learn each part and detail of why, what, and how they are supposed to live and act. Why should we expect children to figure it out even though we would never expect the same kind of automatic understanding from an adult who was untrained in a certain kind of work?

So it is, for example, that an office manager will train a mail room clerk for two weeks before he would expect the new employee to understand the ins and outs of shipping parcels, putting the right postage on envelopes, and stamping the daily incoming mail—pretty basic stuff. At the office the manager trains the clerk and then follows his training up with precisely written-out procedures to follow.

That same training manager then goes home and expects his seven-year-old daughter to automatically understand why she should not have put artichoke leaves down their newly installed sink disposal unit. But the disposal was new, cost money, and the seven-year-old broke it. Her good intentions have little effect on the punishment she receives as a result. And her inability to have known better is not considered at all.

I have known educated, well-mannered adults who managed the affairs of their businesses with the skill of a master communicator—only to go home at night and deal with their own children as though they had left every single communications skill they had ever learned at the office.

As adults, those countless files in the storage room in our subconscious minds serve us well. They give us a wealth of information and experience to go on. We might

147

be confused or unsure now and then, but, for the most part, we have at least some idea of what to do next, regardless of the circumstances at hand.

When we deal with children, we have first to recognize that we are dealing only with what that child's mind has stored. If we fail to recognize this, we tend to *approve of children for what they know and disapprove of them for what they do not know.*

We may do that even when the child had nothing to do with the programs that supplied him with—or didn't give him—the "knowledge" in the first place. We give him credit for storing the programs he has been given, and we shake our head at him for not having the programs that no one gave him—at least not clearly enough—in the first place.

A CHILD'S "BIOLOGICAL" ROAD MAP

Along with the programs he receives, each child also has his own individual genetic chemistry, his biological and neurological makeup. This is a part of the equipment he was born with, and it determines a whole battery of traits and tendencies that, in turn, determine much of who he is.

Some of those inborn genetic traits will affect the speed at which a child is able to learn, a certain amount of his aggressiveness or shyness, a part of his basic level of energy, and a host of chemically preset patterns that will affect much of his feelings and behavior.

Those genetic patterns are like a road map, given to him by his ancestors, that he is unconsciously and biologically persuaded to follow.

148

We become the result of both our genetic conditioning and our external programming. We are not destined from birth to live out a life that is completely predetermined by our genetic heritage, nor do we live out our lives solely on the basis of the programming we receive after we are born. We are a combination of both.

Knowing that helps us to understand, for example, why it is so easy for one child to learn something the first time he is told while another child may have to be taught the same thing in a different way.

UNDERSTANDING A COMPLEX PROCESS—IN A PRACTICAL WAY

As we have seen, a child's mind is a complex mechanism that plays host to a broad variety of paths and programs—which it will do its *best* to *follow*.

When a young boy stands nervously waiting while his mother or father reads the results of his report card from school, he has little idea of the forces that are at play in his life—forces that eventually end up filling in the blanks on that report card and forces that end up filling in a great deal of the details of his life. It is possible that his mother or father do not fully understand those forces either.

As a parent, you can't change the genetic structure that was given to your child. Since the genetic patterns are already there and there is nothing we can do to change them, it will help to recognize them and to help the child build on the best of them.

A NEW WAY TO UNDERSTAND

It is interesting to watch the way different parents talk to their children. You can always tell which of the parents are aware of how a child really thinks and which of them are not.

Those parents who understand talk differently, *listen* differently, and treat their children with a different kind of respect. Parents who are *not* aware of the factors that operate within their children's minds never really figure out what's happening.

Knowing what goes on in a child's mind doesn't always make the job of parenting easier. But it makes it better. More controlled. More rewarding. Understanding the view from the mind of your child gives you the opportunity to share something extra with your child—something that many parents miss entirely.

The next time you talk to your child, think for a moment. Ask yourself the question "What's in his mind?" or "What's in her mind?" Ask yourself who you're *really* talking to. And then ask yourself what you can say that will talk to the *real* person who lives in that mind.

Every chance you get, step inside the incredible mind of the child you care so much about. With that kind of insight, with that kind of understanding, you'll be operating at your best when you set out to get your messages across.

Chapter 14

Getting Your Message Across

I overheard two ladies talking during a break at a seminar I was conducting on Predictive Parenting. One young mother was saying, "I've told Kathy a thousand times, 'No phone call more than fifteen minutes,' and it doesn't make a bit of difference. She's on the phone for hours."

Parents often tell me that they can tell their children something over and over and it still doesn't work. Many parents complain that children just don't listen anymore: "You tell them something and it goes in one ear and out the other." "The more I tell him to be home on time, the less he does it!" "I've pleaded with her until I'm blue in the face, and it still doesn't do any good." "No matter how many times I've told her, she just ignores me."

IF WHAT YOU'RE DOING NOW DOESN'T WORK—CHANGE IT

Sometimes, when they're not getting their message across, parents talk to children in much the same way that people often try to be understood by someone who doesn't speak their language: They talk louder, speak slower, and repeat the same thing over and over—as though that will somehow miraculously, suddenly help them be understood.

A lot of us stubbornly stay with completely ineffective communication styles, even when it is obvious that our style isn't working. *Shouting,* for example, has *never* been a recommended means of communicating with children. And yet shouting is almost a way of life in many households.

Some parents use a different approach. They *coax.* They use any kind of persuasion they can come up with. They will use any form of flattery, promise, or plea necessary to get their children to do what they want them to do. The child has heard it all before, of course, and it didn't work too well then either. But tomorrow the parent will try the same strategy again. And once again it won't work any better than it worked the last time.

Some parents manage by "deals." They bargain for a form of negotiated compliance. Some deals work. But the next deal they make has to be better than the last deal accepted.

The parents hope that in each case they do not end up getting the short end of the deal. And the child learns that a bright mind or a stubborn attitude is worth its weight in chores that he can bargain his way out of doing or report-card grades that will net him a new baseball mitt or extra time off from household duties.

Parents who bargain for compliance are sometimes outdone by other parents who bite the bullet, cut through the negotiations, and go directly to paying hard-earned cash or other awards for the results they are looking for. It is a parenting style that can prove to be expensive, and what they get in return seldom seems to be worth the price.

Some parents opt for the "intellectual sharing" approach to communication and child agreement. This approach does increase understanding among the family members. But some of the proponents of this approach admit that a good, strong authoritative directive such as "Do it now!" would save a lot of time and might actually ensure that the job gets done.

Unfortunately, mixed styles don't tend to work well. When the parent loses intellectual patience, the youngster is still "discussing."

Whether you choose to coax, shout, demand, pay, deal with, or discuss—or all of the above—the question is, "Does it work?"

FUTURE ATTITUDES FROM TODAY'S MESSAGES

To a Predictive Parent, the message is not solely that a child's room gets straightened up; the message is also *"organization."* The message is not only that a child get good grades; the message is *"the value of learning"* and *"the results of effort."* The message is not just that the child should spend less time sitting in front of the television; the message is *"the gift of using time well."*

The message is more than telling a child that he shouldn't yell at his brother; the message is *"the art of getting along with people."* The message is more than being home on time; the message is *"taking responsibility for yourself."*

The primary messages, the things we hear ourselves say most often, help us create a home life that works, one that is reasonably comfortable, happy, and successful.

But in the coming years of a child's life, it is the *secondary* messages that count. And it is the secondary messages that are creating many of the child's *future* attitudes. How well we get *those* messages across is the key.

It is the effect of those secondary messages that will eventually tell us how well we succeeded at our jobs as parents.

If we tell a child that he needs to pay more attention in school, for example, without recognizing that the *real* message is that his own self-discipline will one day be the basis of most of his accomplishments in life, we may get him to pay more attention in school—for a time. But we will not have given him the internal conditioning that *sees* self-discipline as an important quest.

We have to say and do those things that help us manage our homes and lives as smoothly as possible, of course. That means handing out directions, listening and responding, clarifying the guidelines, and dealing with the day-to-day demands of raising kids.

We have to deal with the chores, the report cards, the squabbles, the injured knee, what to order on the pizza, the use of the phone, interruptions, bedtime, and a host of other demands that we face. But somehow, within those demands, also lies the greater purpose and value that we offer as parents.

Along with accepting the realities of day-to-day parenting, it is also important to take a realistic look at how well we get the *rest* of our messages across.

Are you, today, communicating those things to your children that you really *want* to be getting across? Is your style of communicating getting the job done? Are you successfully *reaching* your kids, or are you stuck in a style that isn't working for you?

SOME IMPORTANT QUESTIONS TO ASK YOURSELF

If you would like to make sure that you are getting your messages across, in the right way, the following checklist will help. These are the questions you should ask yourself now and then to keep your parenting communication in good operating shape. Read them to yourself and give yourself clear, simple answers.

I have found that this list of questions works well for raising the level of communication with any child at any age. The purpose here is not to teach "communication." The purpose is to focus on the precise kinds of messages that you would like to deliver to your children, frequently and in the most effective way possible.

If you run across a question that suggests something to you that you need to work on, make a note of it—and work on it. You may want to make a copy of this list and put it on your mirror, where you'll see it every morning. It is a list of questions that most of us would do well to ask ourselves every day we have children in our lives:

How Well Do I Get My Message Across?

1. Do I know what I want to say?

2. Do I take the time to say it?

3. Do I say it every day or every time I should?

4. Do I really let them talk?

5. Do I really listen?

6. Do I understand?

7. Do I let them know that I care what they have to say?

8. Do I take the time to explain?

9. Do I use examples?

10. Do I let them show me they understand?

11. Do I show them "pictures" of themselves being their best?

12. Do I make my message "fun" and interesting?

13. Do I take advantage of every appropriate opportunity I have to get my messages across?

14. Do I get my message across?

If you ask yourself those questions frequently—and work at them—you should be able to get more of your messages across to your children. Also you will be vitally aware that you are actively working at doing it.

You may already be an excellent parent-to-child (or teacher-to-child) communicator, but not everyone is. Some people have spent years communicating the wrong messages. Others have run into a brick wall when they were suddenly faced with getting some of the most important messages of their children's lives across to them.

TWENTY YEARS THAT DIDN'T WORK

I met a grade-school teacher recently who told me that she had spent twenty years *"trying to pound some sense into their heads"* and that during that time *"not more than three or four students out of any class ever listened."* It's no wonder! It is unfortunate that that teacher did not learn, twenty years ago, that "pounding" almost never works! What great things that teacher could have created in more of those young minds if she had only understood.

The parents of three young children told me, "We've tried every punishment in the book, and *nothing* works." I do not have to wonder why. In that case, more "punishment" is not the answer. Those parents will never find their solution by adding more disapproval to the arsenal of negative self-images they have been unwittingly creating in their children's minds.

It is not that punishment is a poor choice of methods— sometimes it is necessary. It is that "deserving punishment" and "low self-esteem" have become the "messages" that those parents most frequently gave.

One mother told me that her house was always "such a madhouse, you can't even hear yourself think." She then asked, "How am I supposed to get my kids to sit down long enough to listen to something good about them when I can't even get them to sit down at the table for dinner?!"

I wonder if that mother, who appeared to have the best of intentions, had ever recognized the value of serving her children a diet of "self-worth" for dinner. Even if they weren't needing food, they were starving for another kind of food that was just as important.

Many parents *know* they have not gotten the right messages across—and eventually, when things get bad enough, they start looking for something they can do to make up for an impoverished past in a parent-child understanding that broke down long ago.

An especially distraught father I met on a speaking tour waited for an opportunity to talk to me privately after I had finished my talk to a group of parents and teachers.

When the father finally got me aside, he told me that his problem was his sixteen-year-old son. "I can't even talk to him anymore," he said. "It's gotten so bad, I've given up trying!" I could not go back to a time, however many years it may have been in the past, when the communication between them first broke down—and neither could he. Whatever messages he had given his son in the past were now causing him more anguish than he dared admit.

SOMETIMES WE DON'T REALIZE THE RESULTS

There are times when a parent simply doesn't realize the negative value that negative beliefs about a child can create. When that happens, most of us would agree that the child in question has little chance of ever reaching the heights he or she was born to reach.

The mother of a twelve-year-old girl called in to a radio talk show I was appearing on in Detroit to ask me, "Why should I tell my daughter any of those *good* things you're suggesting I say? *None of them are true!*"

That mother believed in what she was saying. It *wasn't* true, of course. At least not until she had convinced her daughter that it was. Believing as she did, there is little doubt that the messages she got across to her daughter had already come through loud and clear.

I have wished that I could meet that young girl and talk to her for a while. I have wished even more that her mother could meet her, under far better circumstances, and see in her daughter the wonderful being her daughter so badly needs to be.

In none of those instances was I able to offer any advice that I thought would make much difference. It is difficult to suggest to someone, in only a few minutes without further explanation, that the messages they have been getting across may have been the *wrong* messages.

What is even more unfortunate is that even if those individuals were given a battery of the "right" messages to offer their children, would they know how to get *those* messages across? Or would they, when they were trying to deliver the new messages, use the same styles that had not worked in the past?

That teacher and those parents are in the middle of a quandary and they can't find a way out.

Even with the possibility of help waiting on the threshold, they will not be able to help themselves out of the problem until they recognize that they will have to *first* make a change in how they talk to their kids. They will have to change their message and they will have to change their style of *how* they get their message across.

For some, making that change is just too much to ask. Their own past conditioning is just too strong. For others, even though they *want* to make the change, it will take a test of will.

IF YOUR GOAL IS STRONG ENOUGH

For some of us, getting our messages across will be easier than it will be for others. Some people are less programmed to deny the admission of a new idea or two.

One young single mother of four children attended a seminar I had conducted on "Self-Talk for Parenting." During the seminar I talked about the programming capability of the human mind, and I suggested several specific steps that the attendees could begin using that evening when they went home.

That mother wrote to me several months later. In her letter she told me that that night, following the seminar, she had gone home to a cluttered house, sat her four children down, and repeated for them, in words they could understand, everything she could remember from the seminar that might help them have a home that was "more fun."

After even a few months of working at it, her list of accomplishments was encouraging! She had worked with her children on basic ideas—organization, responsibility, relationships within the family, and cooperation. I especially enjoyed one of her comments: "I know the seminar was supposed to teach me to help my four children learn to do better when they grow up," she wrote, "but I can't believe how much they have 'grown up' already, just by the way I've been working with them."

Most of us, if we will make the decision and take the time to get our real messages across, can succeed. We may have to sweep—or *shovel*—some of our old past programs or parenting out of the way, but if giving our children the messages we would like to give them is important enough, we will do it.

In addition to the points outlined in this chapter that you may want to use to help you do a better job of getting your messages across to your children, I have included, in several of the following chapters, some ideas and methods that should make the job easier for you.

There *are* ways to let our children see incredibly bright, strong, positive, worthwhile pictures of themselves. We usually don't have to make sweeping changes in our lifestyles, throw out old values, or suddenly shock our kids with a whole "new" mom or dad. We can be ourselves.

But we can, at the same time, make a minor adjustment or two. Some of those adjustments we make in the way we talk to our kids will go almost unnoticed by our children. Some of them may come as a refreshing surprise.

Chapter 15

How Long Should It Take?

How long should it take to notice a difference? If you begin communicating in a new way, how long should it take for the new objectives to take effect? If your new words work, when can you expect to see the change take place in your children?

I have often wondered about books on parenting methods that promise immediate results. I would encourage you to be skeptical of any method that promises overnight results. That's not the way the brain works; the mind of a child does not get "changed" miraculously in a day or two, no matter what you do.

If you expect instant results from any new parenting idea, no matter what it is, you will probably be disappointed. And your disappointment is all too good a reason to stop trying.

When we notice a rapid change in a child's attitude or behavior because of some new approach or tack we are taking, that first change is only a temporary response to the new input we are giving the child. But even that new input will not create a lasting change until it is repeated often enough to replace the old programs that the child has stored—programs that may have been years in the making.

Parents often ask me, "If I really work at it, if I do everything I should do to be a Predictive Parent, how long will it take?" Some of the parents who ask me that question are desperate. They have a child who has become difficult. Or they are dealing with a teenager who is getting into trouble.

I would like to tell you that you can start talking and acting in a more positive way and begin to see the results in a few days. But real change takes longer. Can you begin to make a difference starting tomorrow? Yes, you can. But can you create a new set of programs in that child's mind, a set of programs that *last,* in only days or weeks? Experience has taught us that you cannot.

Practicing being a Predictive Parent does not mean that you can solve all of your parenting problems or reach all of your parenting goals as though you had come upon some magic solution. (There is no magic.)

And although Predictive Parenting is a clear and sensible way to work at getting the best results, those results will not be seen in a day or two, or even in a few weeks. The results we work for are often slow in coming. But the results that finally surface are the *real* results that we are working for.

The real objective of parenting is to raise and prepare new adult people who can deal with life in the best possible way. It is to give young people a sense of self, the ability to deal with the inevitable realities of life, and the tools to deal with them.

We may hope for immediate results, but when we are dealing with the mind of a human being, long-term changes almost always come from long-term effort.

EVEN THE FIRST SIGNS OF RESULTS ARE ENCOURAGING

That's not to say that your first week or month or two of modifying your style won't begin to show some signs of positive benefits. You probably *will* notice that even a few days of helping your child see himself in a better light will produce some positive results. And those first results can be encouraging.

Some parents have told me that the first changes they saw in a son or daughter were in some of the most obvious behaviors—getting along better with brothers and sisters, taking more interest in responsibilities at home, or in how they talked and how they listened.

Talking to children in a more Predictive way would be well worth the effort, even if we did it just to improve a few of the attitudes and behaviors that would help make things better *now*. And Predictive Parenting *can* make a noticeable and positive difference in some aspects of your family life, and in school, after even a short time of practicing it.

But the basis of Predictive Parenting is the development of solid, *lasting,* long-term self-identities in the children we are raising. It should not be difficult, then, to recognize that we should look at the results of our parenting over a reasonably long period of time.

CREATING A LIFETIME OF *LONG*-TERM RESULTS

Let's say that you decide to begin tomorrow to develop the highest practical self-identity in your child by practicing, every day, every worthwhile idea and method you can find for adding the best possible pictures and programs to your child's subconscious mind.

When would you expect to see the results? How long would you be willing to work at it before you began to see the lasting, positive results of your efforts?

Your answer to that question is important, because if you expect too much too soon, you could get discouraged and stop trying. On the other hand, if you *know* that Predictive Parenting takes time, you'll give yourself the time you need—and if you're being fair to yourself, you'll also give yourself the *patience* to go along with the time it takes.

The most important of the results we're looking for—the *lasting* results—will not show up in a day, or a week, or sometimes in months.

But then, that is how the life of a child takes shape. It does not change in a moment or two. The life of a child grows and develops step by step, month after month, year after year.

Children do not suddenly become good, or bad, alive with interests or dulled with indifference, prone to good behavior or bent on bad behavior, conditioned for self-fulfillment or conditioned for something less, in a moment of time.

Barring psychological upheavals of catastrophic proportions, the mind of a child is slowly and surely developed and conditioned, moment by moment, day after day, each day and each year of his or her young life.

That is also how they *change*. That is how any change *we* make, in our parenting style, will help *them* change: slowly but surely, moment by moment, day after day.

It is for this reason that I recommend that you work hard in your efforts, create for yourself the best expectations, and exercise patience in evaluating their performance. How well *they* do is a reflection of how well *you* do. Give yourself time, and give them time. It is the *end* result we are going for—not the immediate improvement that we would like to make. It is the *new adult* we are developing—not only the better child we may have during the process.

MEASURING YOUR SUCCESS ALONG THE WAY

To know how well you're doing with the longer-term objective, there are several guidelines you can use to help you recognize how effective your efforts are—both long-term and short-term.

In the following self-evaluation, each of the questions can be answered with a yes or no. You may want to read through them and answer them now and then come back to them in a few weeks or months and ask yourself the same questions again.

1. *I am a better parent today than I was six months ago*...*YES / NO*

2. *I consciously practice Predictive Parenting daily*...*YES / NO*

3. *I can see a difference in how well my child is doing*..*YES / NO*

4. ....*(name of young person) believes herself/ himself to be a unique individual with positive potential*...*YES / NO*

5. *My relationship with my child/children is getting better*..*YES / NO*

6. *I am starting to see a positive difference in my*

family life. Things in general are working better ....*Yes / NO*

7. *My child can talk to me. He or she sees me both as a parent and as a friend*......................*Yes / NO*

8. *I worry about my child/children giving in to harmful outside influences that I can do nothing about*..*Yes / NO*

9. *I feel that I am a positive, respected influence in my child's life* ....*Yes / NO*

10. *My child knows that he/she has exceptional capabilities* ....*Yes / NO*

11. *My child smiles a lot, is happy, and has a healthy, eager, enthusiastic outlook on life* ....*Yes / NO*

12. *If I could do it over again, I would like my child to become the person he/she is becoming* .....*Yes / NO*

It is clear from those questions that none of them could be adequately answered—with progress noted—only a day or two after you made the decision to practice a style of positive Predictive Parenting.

None of the questions address whether or not Kevin's homework is getting done on time or whether or not Ellen is spending too much time with the wrong friends. None of them suggest that you should be raising superchildren or that everything in their—and your—lives should be going along perfectly, without everyday problems.

The questions suggest a broader perspective—a perspective that asks you to look at your progress over a longer period of time and to evaluate your success as a Predictive Parent over a period of months and years, not only in terms of how well you will do tomorrow morning.

The time limit you are dealing with is the life of your child. Your child's success as an individual (and your success as a parent) is not measured only by the achievements or mistakes, positive experiences or difficult times, that happen along the way.

And your child's potential success most *certainly* cannot be projected simply on the basis of some of the problems that he or she might get into now and then. That's only fair. I doubt that many of us would like to show our children an album of photographs of some of the things *we* got into that we "shouldn't have" during the years that we were growing up.

WHAT IF WE NEED TO DO SOMETHING *NOW*?

There are, however, situations that won't wait a few years—or even a few months. We have to do something, and we have to do something *now*.

That situation usually occurs when there is a young person whose life is no longer in control. It could be a teenager who is doing what appears to be everything possible to destroy his or her life, or it could be a younger person who seems bound and determined to create problems and chaos.

Whether you like it or not, you *cannot* suddenly change that young person's identity and programming overnight. We already know that the conditioning part of the brain doesn't work that way.

If you ignore this basic fact of programming, you will end up beating your head against a brick wall. It doesn't make any difference if you would *like* that young person to suddenly change and be different than he or she is. He or she may have unlimited potential and marvelous possibilities somewhere in his or her future—but for now you have to *build,* instead of *fighting,* what is there.

If you have an immediate problem with a young person whose attitude, behavior, or sense of self needs immediate attention, don't expect to change the massive amount of preexisting programs in that young person's warehouse of filing cabinets with an hour of punishment or a day of discipline. It won't work.

When a child or young person is doing something that is decidedly wrong, and is refusing to change, the problem is not the behavior of the moment—the problem is the programmed attitude and conditioning that created the behavior in the first place.

DEALING WITH PROBLEMS THAT COME FROM THE PAST

Most of us have witnessed examples of a parent who is faced with a difficult problem in a young person's behavior that was apparently created by someone else. An example of this is Mark, a father whom I met a number of years ago.

Mark had gained custody of his nine-year-old daughter Jan, who had been living with her mother for five years following their divorce. Jan's conditioning during those five years had been far from the best—and she had found little reason to develop self-esteem. Jan's mother had not had a settled life during the years when she had custody of Jan, and some of Jan's experiences had left noticeable scars in her life—and in her behavior.

The result was that Jan trusted no one, and she wasn't about to accept Mark's parenting, even if a more stable home life might prove to be the very best thing for her development and peace of mind.

Fortunately, Mark recognized that you cannot overcome five years of unhappiness and turmoil in a few short weeks. He proved to be an understanding parent and made the conscious choice to spend the *next* five years—and more—giving Jan the best parenting that he and his new family could offer.

Jan did not instantly respond to her new home. There were a lot of problems that both parents, and Jan, had to work at. Jan had been getting poor grades in school, she had few friends, and she didn't seem to care about her appearance or much else about herself.

But in time, with consistent approval and support from her new family, Jan began to see herself and her life in a more positive light.

Eventually, with love, patience, determination, and an understanding of the new belief Jan needed to find in herself, things got better. In time, Jan began to find a whole new person inside herself. Had Mark demanded a rapid change in Jan's earlier programming, I doubt that it would have worked.

Because her dad and his new family took the time and exercised the patience that "mental program" changes sometimes take, Mark became a successful father and Jan became a successful adult. None of the changes happened overnight. And all of the patience was worth it.

But many of the parenting problems that we face often have less dramatic beginnings than a broken home or an unsettled childhood. Many are surprisingly common. They include behavioral extremes of every kind, imponderable attitudes, and youthful ideas that we will piously state to our own children *we,* even when *we* were young, never *considered.*

By itself, demanding a change in behavior won't solve anything. Jumping on the individual with both feet may scare him or her into submission for a day or two, but it won't last. It can't. The old programs that are causing the problem in the first place are too strong.

If you are dealing with a severe behavioral problem,

get help! There are good therapists and counselors who are trained to give you and the young person some very good advice.

Even the best of positive parenting will not suddenly change someone who has a poor attitude and low self-esteem into a positive, goal-oriented achiever. That takes time.

EVERY POSITIVE NEW PROGRAM CAN HELP

You can help, of course. But if you are trying to solve a problem with a young person today that was created long ago or over a period of time, it will not help to demand changes today.

Every positive addition to that person's programming of self-belief is important. Anything you can do to begin to build that person's self-esteem will give you a better chance than doing or saying anything that will pull that young person's picture of his or her self-identity even lower.

When we are faced with dealing with a young person who has already proved to us that he or she does not like himself or herself very much, we have three options:

1. *We can try to ignore the situation and hope that it will get better. For the time being, it usually won't.*

2. *We can make things worse by voicing our criticism. We don't like what the person is doing, but we often let the person know that we reject more than the behavior—we reject the person. That won't help. Saying something condemning to someone who has already set up a pattern of* *destructive behavior does nothing more than prove to that person that his or her self-concept was correct: worthless, destructive, and unworthy.*

3. *Or we can build on anything we can find in the person that has merit—positive value. And we have to help build that person's wall of self-respect one brick at a time. That's not an easy job. It is hard to build a wall when there may be little or no foundation to build it on in the first place.*

POSITIVE BENEFITS TODAY, EXCEPTIONAL REWARDS TOMORROW

The role of parenting is so much more than that of dealing only with problems, of course. There *are* the joys and the successes along the way—*many* of them. But it can seem at times as though we're making little progress at all and that there are more big problems than little ones. Measuring our success requires some very adult perspectives.

Give yourself time. Don't worry about having to prove yourself or create overnight successes. You don't have to.

If we expect too much change too fast, not only do we think we have failed, we fail our children as well. When we can, it's wise to give our efforts some time to work. Children take time to grow—it's only right that we take the same amount of time to see our best efforts grow along with them.

And the results will come. The child himself will begin to see himself differently, feel better about himself, do better at home, school, with friends—at life in general.

And you'll both recognize the signs of success along the way.

But the greatest reward will come when the child finally becomes the adult, living a life that is filled with the messages you so patiently gave. It is then that you will finally know how well the child learned, and how well your teaching served him.

Imagine, for a moment, your child growing up to be self-confident, happy, and living well. Just imagine knowing that one day that young person may say, "Thank you. You gave me my *self*."

Chapter 16

Discipline, Training, and Punishment

It is sometimes easy to confuse the meaning of these three responsibilities of parenting—*discipline, training,* and *punishment.* They may appear to be similar, but they are separate and distinctly different parenting roles. To better understand why each of these roles is important, let's look at what each of them really means.

DISCIPLINE

To the Predictive Parent or teacher, the word *discipline* takes on a special new meaning. The real meaning of the word (where it came from in the first place) is "to make a disciple of"! In its original form, the word *discipline* does not mean to "punish" or "set straight." It means "leadership"—to discipline is to *lead.*

Understanding what discipline really means can make an important difference to a parent. Knowing that being a good "disciplinarian" means to be a good *leader* gives a new perspective to the role that discipline plays in raising children.

To an aware, Predictive Parent, discipline—leadership—means setting an example. Discipline means accepting the responsibility of showing children, by leading them, how to live, how to act, what to do, what not to do, what works best, how to set internal sights, how to overcome obstacles and problems, how to follow, how to achieve, and in time how to lead.

To be a leader, you have to first be a follower. How anxious your child will be to follow you will depend on how effective a leader you are. If you are a good leader, you will develop good followers.

That doesn't mean that your leadership is designed to create blind adherence—following without thinking. It means that you create, by your own words and actions, an obvious, well-defined example of your direction, your values, and your expectations. And you also create a clear picture of the effects and the *benefits* that will follow as a result of your leadership.

It takes courage to say, "Follow me." When you accept the mantle of leadership in a child's life, you hold in your hands a significant part of that child's future. But isn't that what we do when we become parents? When we decide to have children, we assume the responsibility of *leading* those children through the hurdles of childhood and into the hoped-for self-reliance of adulthood.

The proper use of discipline *should* mean the proper use of leadership. If you see discipline in that way—as leadership—the discipline that you use with your children should work better for you. If, in the past, the word *discipline* has meant to punish, or chastise, give yourself a few days or weeks of practice looking at discipline in its more positive light. You may find that disciplining your children will now prove to be a far more worthwhile and enjoyable experience.

174

TRAINING

Training is similar to discipline, but in some ways it is more direct. To train is to educate—to give knowledge, to *teach*. The Predictive Parent learns that "teaching" children is a specialized job that requires (among other things) five important ingredients:

1. *An acceptance of your responsibility to teach*

2. *The recognition that you are a teacher*

3. *A willingness to constantly learn and try out new ideas*

4. *An interest in finding opportunities to teach*

5. *A dedication to stay with it*

Teaching children takes time. But, far more importantly, it takes your decision to *teach*. When your young son or daughter asks a question, has a problem, or needs guidance, that's not an *interruption,* it's an *opportunity!*

Here are just a few examples of what children say when they are giving us an opportunity to teach them. As you read the examples, think of what some parents might unknowingly say in response and consider what a conscientious Predictive Parent (one who knows he or she is the child's number-one teacher) might offer instead:

"Will you leave the light on, I'm scared?" "I don't understand . . . " "Why can't I go?" "What makes the car work?" "What's wrong with it?" "I didn't do anything," "I just can't do it," "Can't you just write a check?" "I didn't break it," "I can't find my baseball," "I don't have to study that, it's not going to be on the test," "You didn't tell me I had to be home," "Do I have to?" How do you get to be the president?" "What does NASA mean?" "Will it hurt?"

"None of the other kids have to," "My teacher doesn't like me," "It's not fair," "She wore my bracelet without asking," "All the kids talk like that," "If I have to figure something out, I can use a calculator," or "I don't like him, he talks funny."

In even that short selection of comments and questions that come from children, the parent is offered a wealth of teaching opportunities.

In response to just those few examples you could, if you chose, offer your thoughts, your ideas, your *teaching* on: safety and security, personal responsibility, automotive engineering, self-confidence, organization, education, schedules, politics, the space program, preventive medicine, parental authority, the importance of good grammar, the problems of teaching school, fairness, sharing, the reason for math, and recognizing prejudice.

There are, in most of our homes, more opportunities for teaching than there is time available. But as a parent, you *are* your child's number-one teacher. Deciding to teach, and taking the time to teach, can create a bond—and an understanding—that will last throughout your child's entire life.

Do you explain to a child the sorrow you feel when someone close to you has died? Do you tell him something more about the rainbow in the sky, after an evening rain, than he will learn from his science class at school?

What do you teach your child? What is your child getting from *you* that he or she could not possibly get, in the same special way, from anyone else but you?

Teaching your child is a great responsibility. Taking the time to teach is an almost untold investment in your child's future. But it is even more than that. It is one of the greatest *opportunities* you will ever have as a parent.

PUNISHMENT

Last comes punishment—and it should come last. In most cases, the need for punishment is the result of too little discipline (leadership) and, at times, too little, or the wrong kind of, training. The more effective you are at being a leader, setting an example, and taking the time to teach, the less you should have to rely on punishment because of the results of bad behavior.

As parents, we deal with different kinds of punishment. One of them is the kind of punishment we use when a child or young person has to learn the results of the wrong kind of behavior. It is a way of teaching responsibility: "If you do something wrong, you have to pay the price." If it is the *right* kind of punishment, then the punishment is a *lesson*—and we hope that the punishment does its job and that the bad behavior will not be repeated.

Another kind of punishment is presented to children or teenagers as a deterrent. It is a kind of *potential* punishment, which is held up to the child as the "worst case" possibility and one which the parent never expects to exercise.

There are times when some form of punishment is entirely appropriate. But it is important to recognize that punishment is a last resort—it is what you have to do when everything else you have tried has failed.

The meaning of the word *punishment,* to a Predictive Parent, is to *correct.*" And to correct a child, in the most worthwhile way, means to help the child improve the *choices* he makes, instead of relying on penalties to prove to him what doesn't work.

There are times when the penalty may be necessary, but even more important is the child's understanding of "personal choice."

Helping a child or young person correct his behavior—

177

when seen from the perspective of showing him his best—is taking the time to give him the feedback he needs about the choices he makes and showing him why his choices are important—so that he can do it better next time.

When we punish a child, if we are being fair with him, it is always because the child has made a "wrong" choice. Even though the child or young person often believes that it is the act itself that got him into trouble, it is really the *choice* he made that created the problem.

It is for this reason that when you consider punishment, keep in mind the fact that the real objective is to give your child the understanding to make better *choices*.

When your child does something wrong, something that deserves or demands punishment of one kind or another, when you make your decision about what to do about it, also ask yourself the question "What caused him, in his mind, to make the choice he made that caused the problem?"

Then, in whatever you decide to do next, don't tackle only the behavior. Discuss with him or her what created the choices that created the behavior—in the first place.

If the punishment you choose to use gives your child or young person an understanding of why a different choice might work better, you will increase your chances of not having to repeat the same punishment again.

The kind of "punishment" that almost always works best—in the long run—is the kind of guidance that teaches the value, the skill, and the importance of making good choices. When we do that, we give the child more of the understanding he needs to help him make better choices for himself, in the future.

THE FAR-REACHING EFFECTS OF "GUIDANCE"

Together, these three parenting tools—discipline, training, and punishment—make up much of what we call guidance. Used in the right way, *predictively,* these tools can help us form many of the first positive paths that our children will follow. The effects of them will reach well beyond the few short parenting years our child will have.

To the Predictive Parent, *discipline* means leadership. *Training* is teaching. And *punishment* is the improvement of the ability to make good choices.

When we lead, teach, and help children improve their choices, with their best potential in mind, we are literally guiding them along paths that will give them the best chances for growth and success.

Chapter 17

Dealing with the Rest of the World

As parents, we cannot hide our kids away from the rest of the world—we can't keep them locked safely away in a castle tower, out of reach of all of the possible negative influences that surround them.

We cannot demand that they stop listening to the wrong kind of advice or suddenly stop being influenced by the wrong kind of socially advocated opportunities that tug at their minds.

We can't put our children's minds on a leash. And we most certainly cannot sit them down for an hour or two and give them a talk about wrong influences and expect our few words of wisdom to suddenly override whatever previous conditioning, to the opposite, they already have.

We can't be there with our child every moment of every day to make sure that he or she makes the right choices.

While you embark on a program of giving your own child the strongest possible internal influences, how do you combat the influences that surround your child and are outside your control?

How do you make your programs stick, and what can you do to make sure that your programs of positive direction and self-belief for your child are not overridden or replaced by the normal everyday input of negative programming?

How do you deal with the *rest* of the world? You can't ignore it, you can't turn off the television, stop the music, get your children to divorce their friends or refuse to send them to school. One way or another, our children are going to have to live in the society that surrounds us.

But while living in that society, how can you somehow create an environment of nurturance for your child that will set him or her apart from outside negative influences? What can you do *today* that will make a difference?

SOME OF THE INFLUENCES OUR CHILDREN FACE

There is a lengthy list of outside influences that our children face in the few short years that we have to raise them; during that period we hope that we ourselves will provide the most lasting influences of all. Let's break this down into a smaller list of groups of influences that affect our children—and thereby us.

If we learn what the real influences are, which of them we should be concerned with, and which of them will likely not leave a lasting impression, we can more easily deal with each of them—either in advance or when they eventually crop up.

1. Influences That Cause Short-Term Problems but Have Little Lasting Effect

Among these are fads; youth-oriented "dress codes"; new forms of speech (expressions that are "in"); passing, short-term friends and acquaintances; and popular pastimes.

We all had them. The effect on our lives, at the time, may have seemed profound. But in time, each of these influences gave way and some other event or some newer interest took its place.

These outside influences can cause parents to throw up their hands in defeat; but few of them are strong enough to create lasting effects, and most deserve little more from parents than the wisdom of knowing that "This too shall pass." Fortunately, most of them do.

2. Influences That Have a Long-Term Impact on Your Child's Beliefs and Perceptions

These influences include school (both inside the classroom and out); the media (including television, newspapers, magazines, etc.); movies; books; acquaintances and longer-term friends; cliques and groups; social mores; and other affiliations, organizations, and activities outside the home.

Some of these are more important than others—they affect our children in different ways, with differing degrees of seriousness. But each of these areas of influence deserves more of our parenting attention and concern than the ones in the previous group. It is these influences that take up a large percentage of our children's time—and their minds.

They have added importance in that they shape beliefs, attitudes, and behaviors that, if strong enough, will stay with a child or young person for a long period of time—sometimes for life.

Many of these influences are beneficial. Some of them are not. *All* of them deserve our attention and our judgment. Anything that could have a lasting effect on our children's self-identities is a matter of parental responsibility and choice.

3. Influences That Contradict the Values or Teachings That You Hold Important

Any of the influences mentioned previously could, if they were significant, fall into this category. This group is made up of situations that create problems for us because they potentially establish beliefs or ideals for our children that are contrary to our own.

These include the philosophical points of view (which we may not agree with) that are raised by political organizations, religious teachings (outside our own), culturally imposed moral or ethical standards that may be in conflict with our or other standards of behavior that may be acceptable to many but are not in keeping with the beliefs we as parents choose to adopt or adhere to.

These would include whatever affects and shapes our children's attitudes and beliefs on such issues as war, welfare, social responsibility, the importance of personal wealth and gain, and the individual meaning and importance of commonly accepted norms of social success and failure.

It is this category of outside influences that would also include "concepts" of parenting, what values should be imposed, which traditions are important, and which are not (concepts that, I should point out, are *not* taught or suggested in this book).

The influences in this category come from a broad variety of sources and are usually not identifiable as coming from a single source. They are just one more set of factors that we should recognize as being strongly influential in our children's lives and minds.

I am not suggesting, of course, that we should attempt to keep our children in a newly imposed form of social "dark ages," unaware and ignorant of what is being taught in the world around them. Far from it.

But I am suggesting that each of us recognize and be

well informed about values and beliefs taught outside the home that may not be to our liking.

As parents, it is not only our right to recognize and deal with the influences that affect our children, it is our responsibility.

4. Influences That Are Potentially Destructive or "Problem-Creating" in Nature

This is perhaps the toughest group of influences of all, because they seem to create the greatest problems, the greatest heartaches. These are the influences that snuff out young lives or cripple future happiness just when a young life seems to be beginning. They seem actually to take away a child's love, trust, or belief; to involve a young person in irresponsible activities such as drug abuse, drinking, reckless driving, skipping school, or dropping out. They include the influence of *any* person (or group) who would attempt to dominate the minds of our children at a time when those young minds have not yet learned to direct and dominate themselves.

5. Influences That Are Positive and Productive

Fortunately, these are the influences that can, if we look for them, still make up the longest list of all.

This list includes good friends; solid, well-planned educational programs in school; an awareness of the freedom to experience and learn; a wealth of proven traditions and time-tested values even from the outside world; television and the media (seen here in its more positive, enlightening role); involvement in positive, productive, personal-growth-oriented organizations and group activities; churches and other potential-developing spiritual pursuits; and a world of motivationally inspiring, life-changing influences and directions from literature, the arts, involvement in sport, *and the exceptional influence of positive personal experience.*

THE NATURAL LAWS OF THE SUBCONSCIOUS MIND

There may be more *good* influences around our children than *bad*. That is part of what we, as Predictive Parents, look for—and find. As Predictive Parents finding the winning qualities in life instead of dwelling on the insurmountable problems, we seek out those influences that help our children and learn to deal with—and outsmart, or *outinfluence*—those factors that threaten to pull them down.

It is when we clearly understand what to do about outside influences that we do our best in helping our children overcome or get past them.

We can't ignore the rest of the world—and it certainly isn't going to suddenly change or go away. The answer lies in one of the "rules" of the subconscious mind: It is a characterisic of our subconscious that:

The strongest programs win out.

And the subconscious mind always attempts to act on the strongest programs it holds.

When two subconscious programs are in conflict with each other, one of the two will usually be stronger, and that is the program that will end up directing or affecting the young person's beliefs, attitudes, emotions, and behavior.

Another characteristic of the programming process of the subconscious mind states:

The strength of the program is affected by the number of times the same or similar information is presented.

185

The more often a young person hears the same thing, the greater the chance that he will complete a file in his subconscious mind that agrees with what that program has told him.

This explains why a teenage boy who spends two hours a week at home (during waking hours) and fifty hours a week in the company of friends will adopt so many programs that come from the friends rather than from his parents. Those "outside" programs are stronger and are repeated to his subconscious mind more frequently.

In addition to other important psychological motivations, one of the reasons peer-group pressure and influence are so strong is that they represent an incredible amount of external *programming* for the child or young person. Even the best, most caring "files" that you add to your child's mind can be overridden, over*powered,* by other programs that are stronger.

A third rule of the programming process of the mind states:

The strength of a program is influenced by the value or importance of the program source.

How much you believe or trust in the person who is influencing you will strongly affect how much influence that person can have in your programming.

The subconscious mind does not, by itself, select where *any* of its programs come from. It simply accepts them all and acts on the strongest of them.

The programming process of the subconscious mind follows very specific rules. Whether we like it or not, a mind *does* get programmed and it *does* respond to the strongest programs it receives.

If you are aware of that fact, you will not have automatically won the battle, but you will give yourself a better chance of remaining in control of at least *some* of the strongest influences that your young person receives.

There are those in our society who would, if they could, control every part of our children's minds. They would control and manipulate our children for their own purposes.

You can be sure that there are those who understand, all too well, how a young person's mind is programmed and influenced. And they use that knowledge to wreak havoc with young lives.

THE SAME RULES CAN HELP US

Once you understand how the *process* works, you give yourself a better chance of beating them at their own game. Since the subconscious mind *does* follow "rules of programming," we might just as well make those programming rules *for* us.*

Aware of it or not, the minds of our young are battlefields on which a fight for control is raging. The goal is the life and future of that young boy or girl.

It isn't just cult groups or fanatical organizations that wage the war for the minds of the young. Children's minds are grasped for from every side: Advertisers want their buying power. Schools want their attention. Religions want their faith. Schoolmates want their friendship, and parents want their love, obedience, and respect.

Some of the players in this tug-of-war for young minds sincerely want the best for that young person. Much of what they have to offer is good and worthwhile. What they give in return for the mind they attract will benefit the young person.

The influences of negative human motives *do* exist—

*For a complete list of the Programming Rules of the Subconscious Mind, see Shad Helmstetter's *The Self-Talk Solution*, Simon and Schuster, Pocket Books.

and we should be aware of them. But fear, paranoia, and anger, are not the solutions. You should know, for instance, that a human brain is not won over quite so easily as some would have us believe.

The battle for a mind is not won or lost in a few moments or a few words. The programming and conditioning process of the subconscious mind is a long, slow building process. Some programs—some words or experiences—will affect it more immediately and more profoundly than others, but the entire structure of a mind is years in the making.

When we hear of some young person who has been swept away overnight and transformed instantly from a normal healthy, happy young person into a devoted follower of some fanatical belief, you can be sure that the conversion *of his subconscious mind* did not happen overnight.

There may have been a final moment of "submission" (that *appears* to be a conversion), but the preparation and the programs that led up to that moment were much longer in the making.

No one has a hypnotic spell that can suddenly—*without prior preparedness*—blind and bind any of us. No one has the power to suddenly walk into the filing center of a young person's subconscious mind, pull all of the millions of files that are stored there, sweep them out, and replace them with *an entire new set of programs* in a moment or a day.

The brain simply doesn't work that way. If it did, *we* could use the same broom to sweep out anything that is causing *us* a problem and instantly replace it with something better!

Anyone who would like to control (or influence) your child's mind has to follow the same "rules" of the mind that we have to follow. Those rules correspond to basic physiological and neurological facts of the physical brain that holds the mind within it.

What we say when we talk to our kids is not the final "cure" for the cultural problems our kids face today. But our determined support in helping them build a strong sense of self, strong self-esteem, is one of the most important things that *we* can do.

Our own words and actions help our children and young people create their "first line of defense"—to prepare, guard, and protect them from the very real problems that outside negative influences *will* attempt to create in their lives.

Consider what files that young person might need that will teach him to question—to "look before he leaps"—to assess right and wrong and eventually to choose.

BUILD A LINE OF FIRST DEFENSE

To change attitudes and beliefs, you must first change the programming. To change the programming from the old to the new, you have to create a message that is stronger, more powerful, more *chemically active* in the brain, than the earlier programs that are already on file.

If a young person in your life is being led down the wrong path by some other influence in his life, look *first* at what files he may already have that are healthy and strong—that you and the young person can use to build on. When you do this, you are creating a program of *pre*-defense—a form of internal self-defense.

Practice using the kind of Parent-Talk that we discussed in Chapter 11. Start using Self-Talk (Chapter 19) that helps create a new pattern of self-directions in the mind and let the person know how the process works.

Use every opportunity to help the child or young person build a line of first defense. Build it consciously and let him know what you're doing. Talk about it. Discuss it. Bring the problem out into the open. And work on the goal together.

CHILDHOOD "BLUES" OR LONG-TERM *INDIFFERENCE?*

Another kind of programming that is often less obvious, and yet potentially just as destructive to a child's potential, is the programming of *indifference*—complacency and mediocrity, a sense of "averageness" in a young person's internal picture of himself.

A child's feeling of a sense of "belonging," being "part of the group," is one thing. But a self-belief that keeps a young person from rising above the crowd is something else entirely. An attitude that demands little more of one's *self* than that he "get along," or "get by," with as few ripples and waves as possible, will never create a fulfilling life for anyone.

These attitudes come to our children in the form of a seemingly normal prevailing attitude of unattended youth. It is an attitude that can flourish in front of us without setting off our parental alarms because it appears to be harmless. It can seem to be nothing much more than a "natural" way for kids to be.

But what are the attitudes that create long-term happiness; self-sufficiency; self-belief; a positive, winning life-style; and a life of taking personal responsibility for one's own successes? Certainly not the attitude of indifference or getting by.

The problem is that the mind of a child who has learned to get by, go along with the crowd, or indifferently fall in step with whatever is happening will naturally be most susceptible to the influences of the world around him.

This is not a case where someone is trying to program him with the wrong information or give him files that will slow him down or hold him back. The problem is that young person is not aware of the programs that are being fed to him. And he is even less aware of the relationship between those thousands of unnoticed files and the effect they will create.

A prevailing attitude of indifference in the mind of a young person means that the strongest mental programs that are in operation at the moment are incomplete, soft, vague, or contradicting programs.

The result is that the child leaves himself wide open to accept the strongest new programs that come his way—whether they are healthy, positive influences or influences of the mentally *un*healthy, negative kind.

THE FILES WILL FILL WITH WHATEVER THEY'RE GIVEN

Seventeen or eighteen years or so is a lot of time to fill a lot of files. Since life today is pretty complex, a lot of questionable stuff is being thrown our kids' way. As we have learned, the subconscious mind will accept whatever is programmed into it—if it is programmed often enough and strongly enough—*whether or not the information it receives is true, false, right, wrong, bad, or good.*

Understanding that, it is easy to see why a vague, indifferent, nonselective storage center in the mind will all too easily accept outside programs or influences that *we* as parents know are the wrong kind, even though the child being influenced doesn't really know what is happening to him. Simply *telling* him to be more careful won't make the difference.

RECOGNIZE, ANALYZE, AND TAKE ACTION

What, then, is the solution? An important part of the answer is a conscious shift in some of what we say when we talk to our kids—not now and then, but consistently, over a period of time.

Look at the influences, know what they are, recognize what effects they'll have—and take action!

The right kind of Predictive Parenting can have a direct and positive influence that can stop for now, and forestall in advance, some of the negative influences our children encounter—*before* too many of those influences have a chance to dig in, take root, and grow on their own.

Our best defense against the negative influences that will come to kids along the way is to prepare them now with the strongest positive programs of our own that we can give them. When we do this, we are preparing them to *win*.

Chapter 18

Setting Them Up for Success

It is becoming increasingly apparent, from our study of the human mind, that when we parent, we either set our children up for success or we end up leaving most of it to the future—and hoping for the best.

Many parents still trust in "luck" when it comes to the futures of their children. There may be some fortunate opportunities involved along the way as our youngsters go through life, but luck will never determine the success of any of them.

Rather than hoping for the best, hoping for luck, or leaving their futures up to chance or the whims of the rest of the world, it makes a lot more sense to *prepare* our children for success. *Get them ready for it. Condition them for it. Help them learn to expect it.* And show them that "success," and the creation of it, has always started with a state of mind.

I'm not speaking here of something as ordinary as financial success or the successes that are tied to a position or a career. I'm talking about the success of *self* that each of us wants and needs as individuals—whatever shape or form it may take. It is that overriding success of mind that makes the other social successes possible.

I have known people who wanted more than anything else to be successful in their jobs or careers. I have known others who have placed success at home above all other successes. Still others have wanted to achieve success in expressing themselves—speaking, writing, thinking, building, managing—or some other worthwhile endeavor.

We have all known people who believe that the measurement of success is the accumulation of some amount of material wealth. We have known others who measured their own success by the class of friends who accepted them. Others have measured their success by their prominence—their leadership or their social standing.

Any of those measurements of success can be worthwhile. They serve their purpose. They give people challenges to work for and they reward the achievers with a sense of accomplishment and value.

But beyond the more commonly accepted measurements of success, there is clearly another kind of success, one that does not rise and fall with the attainment or loss of wealth or standing. It is a kind of success that is almost indifferent to setbacks and obstacles. It is not built up one day and lost another. It stays.

This special kind of success is not won by merit, conferred by authority, determined by someone else, or awarded for achievement. It is instead a kind of success that lives within the mind. It is a success that is felt rather than measured, a success that is a part of the foundation of a well-formed *self*.

This special kind of success is unimaginably important. It is the perspective from which all other successes in anyone's life are created, identified, and accepted. Without it, the greatest wealth or position has little worth. With it, the smallest detail of life has meaning and value.

The assessment of this kind of success comes only from the person—*inside*.

THE KIND OF SUCCESS THAT HAPPENS IN THE MIND

True, lasting success is a state of mind. It is interesting that those individuals who are most apt to make that comment—and live by it—are most usually people who are in their seventies or eighties. They have lived a lot of life, had a chance to see it from a lot of sides, had their "successes" and their "failures," and finally figured out what real success was all about.

Part of that success comes from a well-defined sense of self-esteem. Part of it comes from a kind of confidence that lets us know that we can overcome the bad and get on with the good. Part of it comes from an internal sense of security that assures us that *we're* okay, even when other things are not.

And part of it comes from an understanding that we, as individuals, have a worth that can never be fully measured by the outside circumstances of day-to-day living; it is measured not by the car we drive, what we do for a living, how handsome or pretty we are, how much money we have in the bank, or how well we scored on an achievement test at school.

Many parents agree that it is a good idea to do everything possible to help their children reach the greatest heights of their potential successes. But we would neglect an important part of our children's preparation if we did not also teach them about the kind of success that will, if they recognize it, create for them a greater sense of well-being than any other "success" in life that they will ever achieve.

THE SUCCESS THAT CANNOT FAIL

When you set your children up for success, when you prepare their young minds to expect and go for the best of themselves, always remember that there is a part of each of them that needs to know that, with or without the external successes in life, he or she is, and always will be, a marvelous and exceptional human being.

The external successes our children learn to create for themselves will become an important part of their futures. Some of those successes will help them build self-esteem, self-confidence, and a sense of pride in who they are and how well they live out the opportunities and the problems in their lives.

It is those successes, the *external* kind, that we will usually find ourselves working hardest to help them create.

But if we want to set our children up—prepare them—for the success that will stay with them the longest and help them find value in the other external successes they create, we should also help them set up the quiet, internal kind of success.

That is the success that rises above, and lives beyond, all other successes.

When we get a phone call from our son or daughter, some Mother's Day or Father's Day a few years from now, after he or she is grown, most of us would like to hear something more than words, "Thanks, Mom", or "Thanks Dad, I'm successful." Above all, most of us would love to hear the words, *"I'm happy."*

The internal sense of peace and fulfillment that we call happiness will always be the true measure of our children's success. And as parents, how well we helped them *find* it will always be the measure of ours.

Chapter 19

The Powerful Programs of Self-Talk

One of the most effective methods we've found to help us with the job of Predictive Parenting is to teach our kids to use Self-Talk.

Self-Talk is a method that anyone can use—even a small child—to replace or override negative programs with self-directed words of positive self-direction.

Self-Talk is especially helpful to kids because Self-Talk uses the exact same process that the brain uses *naturally* to create programs in the mind.

When a child hears a negative remark from a classmate at school, for example, what will she automatically say to herself in her mind? What *message* will the negative comment from the classmate *imprint* in the subconscious mind of the child who hears it?

And even more importantly, *what protective words of positive Self-Talk will already be in place in the young girl's mind to override the negative program she is being given?*

When someone is trying to persuade a young person to do something that is irresponsible or "the wrong thing to do," what strong mental programs or influences will that young person already have in place, in his mind that will help him say no?

Self-Talk is a way of teaching young people some of the most basic programs of self-direction, programs that are strong, memorable, and immediately usable.

Imagine, for instance, a young boy who is at home in the evening working at his homework. He's having trouble staying with it, and there is a good chance that unless he receives some encouragement fairly soon, he'll quit and go on to something else.

If that youngster wants to get his homework done but lacks the initiative to stay at it, his own (previously learned) internal Self-Talk at the moment will often make the difference between getting his homework done and turning it in late.

The right kind of Self-Talk also helps children and young people with a host of other internal files—such as *attitude, personal organization, habits, enthusiasm, personal responsibility, dealing with problems,* and *self-esteem,* among others.

A CLEAR FOCUS—ON POSITIVE PICTURES

Self-Talk helps young people "focus" on specific areas of personal growth and gives them clear, understandable words and pictures that help create positive influences in their minds.

Self-Talk is not difficult to teach, because it is easy to learn. Young people, of almost any age, pick it up naturally because they are learning their new positive Self-Talk the same way they are learning the other internal programs that come to them.

Because Self-Talk works the way the mind works, learning Self-Talk is no different from learning anything else. But the words and the internal influences that a child's new Self-Talk is giving him are much stronger—and much more positive than many of the other programs he receives.

A child's Self-Talk can be a single phrase or it can be a group of phrases, all of which work together to create a precise mental picture of himself that lets him see himself doing better or achieving the goal.

Self-Talk is *positive influence* in one of its most direct and effective forms. Positive Self-Talk takes the best of a child's potential and presents it to him in simple, straightforward statements of fact.

BUILDING AN INTERNAL PICTURE OF SELF-BELIEF

The right kind of Self-Talk for a young person says, "*This* is who you are—this is who you are capable of being!" And it repeats that same message to a child often enough that the child's mind begins to get the picture, accepts it, and makes *that* picture an active, working, *believing* part of everyday life.

For example, here is a script of Self-Talk phrases that many parents and teachers have used with children. It is a script of Self-Talk that deals with self-esteem, that is, developing a strong, healthy internal attitude about themselves.

POSITIVE SELF-TALK FOR SELF-ESTEEM FOR CHILDREN

I like myself. And other people like me too.

I like who I am and I like how I look. I like the person I see when I look in the mirror.

I smile a lot. I am happy and I feel good about myself.

I like the people I live with. I love them and care about them, and they love and care about me too.

I like learning to do things. I like learning things at home and learning things at school.

Every day I learn more and every day I do more things by myself.

I always think good things about myself.

I take good care of my things. And I am always careful with things that belong to someone else.

I like to keep my room neat and clean and I am proud of myself for keeping it that way.

I am a good friend. I like to be around other people, and they like to be around me.

I know that I can become anything I want to in my life. I am very special, and I make my best dreams come true.

I am good at following directions and doing things right.

I am glad that other people care about me and take the time to teach me what to do and how to do it.

I would rather be friendly than argue or fight. Being nice to others is important to me, and I always get along well with my family and friends.

I enjoy helping others and I like doing things together.

I am a very good listener. I pay attention to what people say, and because I do, they pay attention to me too.

Every day I am getting a little older, a little taller, and a little better in everything I do.

I like who I am and I'm glad to be me!

Most children learn Self-Talk of that kind by listening to it on cassette tapes (which you can obtain commercially recorded or record for your children yourself). Another way that kids learn Self-Talk is by reading it each day, written out on cards.

THE SPECIAL WORDS OF SELF-TALK

You'll notice that all of the Self-Talk phrases are written in the *present* tense and in first person. They are important messages *from* the child *to* the child, stated in the present tense to give him a *completed* picture of how he can be, as though he already is the way he's picturing himself to be in his mind.

The Self-Talk statements are worded in a specific way so that a child's subconscious mind will hear the words as a specific direction that says, *"This is how I want to be. This is how I am!"* Self-directions worded in that way create stronger, more specific pictures in a young person's mind.

If a child's Self-Talk told him instead that he is *going to do well in school* or that he *would like to* get along better with his brothers or sisters, the message he would give to his subconscious control center would be, "Do it in the future . . . at some other time."

The more clearly a child or a young person sees himself having already accomplished the goal, the sooner his new Self-Talk will help him make sure that that is the way he is already becoming.

When a child begins to use Self-Talk that paints a picture of himself or herself as "being on time," "being a good listener," "able to concentrate," or "getting along well with friends and family," he is not fooling himself by putting those positive pictures of himself in his mind. He is simply creating a stronger picture of an attitude or ability that was inherently within him all along.

The Self-Talk just serves to bring it out into the open, concentrate on it, allow the mind to work on it, accept it, and act it out.

HOW YOUNG PEOPLE LEARN SELF-TALK

Children do not learn Self-Talk by memorizing it as they would learn a poem or an essay or a list of presidents. They learn it by hearing it, reading it, writing it, or practicing it in some other way—and being taught that it is a truth about *them.*

It is not just the words they are hearing or giving themselves that are important—it is the messages they are repeating to some very important storage files in their subconscious minds that make Self-Talk work.

This same form of Self-Talk is now being used by families in their homes, and by classroom teachers in schools throughout the United States.*

The benefits and the results that are being experienced by people who use it are sometimes amazing. Imagine raising a child to recognize and reinforce those incredible, positive truths about himself or herself. Imagine what the results of that kind of self-belief might create in that young person's life today—and in his or her future tomorrow.

Here is another example of Self-Talk. This Self-Talk script was written for teenagers. Some of the words and thoughts are different from those in the earlier example—because this Self-Talk speaks to young people of a different age. But the words deliver a similar message to the mind of the young person who hears them.

POSITIVE SELF-TALK FOR TEENS

I have the ability and the right to achieve and do well in my life. I'm more than just okay. I am a *winner*!

I believe in myself. I trust in who I am. I may listen to the ideas and suggestions of others, but when it comes right down to it, I believe in myself and in all of the potential I have within me.

I respect myself and I like who I am. I'm pretty special, and the more I recognize that fact about myself, the more others recognize that it's *true*!

People *like* me. I am courteous, kind, thoughtful, and considerate. These are just a few of the traits

* For information on "Self-Talk Programs for Schools," write to the Self-Talk Institute, P.O. Box 5165, Scottsdale, Arizona 85261.

that I possess that will benefit and reward me for the rest of my life.

My word is golden. I can be counted on. What I say I will do, I always do. And I only agree to those things that are healthy, helpful, and beneficial to myself and to others.

By making the decision to win in my life, I have become one of those who decide to achieve the best. I deserve the best from *myself,* and the best is what I get!

I see personal responsibility as the beginning of all success. I take responsibility for myself and everything I do—and it shows!

I take responsibility for every thought I think. I know that what I think directs and affects everything else about me.

I choose to think only those thoughts that guide, support, direct, and enrich my life and the lives of others in the most positive possible way.

I set goals for myself. I see myself reaching my goals. Each day I see my goals—and my future—more clearly.

I believe in working hard and doing things right! I believe in achieving the best from myself. I know that I can achieve any goal I choose.

I am a doer, an achiever, a worker, and a winner! I have mastered the skill of liking myself.

I know that I can do anything I believe I can do. So I set my sights, and I do it. Today especially! I believe in myself and I'm going for it!

I am ready. I am responsible for my actions and my successes. I accept that responsibility. I'm pretty good already—and I'm just getting started.

I am a winner! Just watch me, and I'll *prove* it!

Imagine what a young person might do with his life with that much sense of *self*. There is no telling what a young person with those self-beliefs could do.

If you examine each of the Self-Talk phrases in the examples we have used here, the message is clear: A young person who thinks like *that* is a young person who will set himself up for more success—more personal fulfillment in life—in whatever he or she chooses to do.

PRACTICING SELF-TALK AT HOME

There is no end to the Self-Talk that a young person or a child can use. You may want to purchase prerecorded Self-Talk cassette tapes and play them for your children. Or you may want to help your child write his *own* Self-Talk and record his own words for him. (If you decide to make your own cassettes instead of playing prerecorded Self-Talk tapes, your tapes will work best if you record a voice other than that of your child's voice on the cassettes.)

Self-Talk on cassettes is especially effective because the tapes can be played almost anytime. They work best when they are played frequently, so the more often your child listens to them, the more they'll help.

In addition to using Self-Talk on tapes, the best way for a young person to learn Self-Talk is for you to practice it in your home—for yourself and with your kids. Listen to it. Talk about it. Explain it. Use it. And encourage it. When you do that, Self-Talk becomes a regular part of your everyday life—and your child's.

The more naturally you adopt Self-Talk as a part of your home life, the more easily your children will pick it up, try it for themselves, and begin to apply it to their everyday lives.

All of us have enough of the other kind—the negative kind—of the self-talk of self-*doubt* to deal with. Positive Self-Talk of the self-believing kind will help your child balance out the rest of the self-talk that may already be a part of his own unconscious directions to himself.

SELF-TALK FOR BETTER ATTITUDES AND SELF-TALK FOR SPECIAL SITUATIONS

When you are teaching Self-Talk to your children, there are two forms of Self-Talk that have the strongest and most immediate effect. One of them is *Self-Talk for Building Attitudes*. That is the form that the earlier Self-Talk examples deal with most.

The other form of Self-Talk deals with specific problems or situations *right now*. That is called Situational Self-Talk. I'll give you an example.

A mother told me the story of her seven-year-old daughter Emmaleigh, who was getting ready to enter second grade and was worried about doing well because she hadn't learned some of her basic math tables. When she shuffled through the pack of flash cards for adding, subtracting, multiplying, and dividing, she panicked when she realized she had forgotten most of them.

Her mother had been using Self-Talk tapes with her kids at home, and each of them had learned some positive Self-Talk by listening to those tapes. When a specific problem arose, the mother would suggest a phrase or two of Situational Self-Talk that her children could use to help themselves fix the problem.

So the mother asked Emmaleigh what Self-Talk she could think of to help her concentrate and learn her tables. Emmaleigh asked, "What if I tell myself that learning my tables is easy and I can learn them fast?"

Her mother agreed that that would be excellent Self-Talk to use for the situation, and Emmaleigh and her mother began to go through each of the flash cards, with Emmaleigh repeating out loud, between each of them, "This is easy and I am learning fast."

Her mother told me that an hour later, she had never seen her daughter more excited! Emmaleigh was doing cartwheels on the living room floor, she was so happy and proud of herself. It worked! By *convincing* herself that she could do it, and by using the Self-Talk to open up all of the ready-and-waiting internal support systems in her subconscious mind, she *did* it!

The important message here is that it was not some magic formula that little Emmaleigh called into play to help her with her math. By using very specific Self-Talk—*self-directions*—Emmaleigh, almost unknowingly, called into play some of the most powerful focusing skills of the human brain, and her brain responded accordingly; she told it what to do, and it did it.

That story would come as no surprise to any NASA-trained astronaut, or even most commercial airline pilots. Our most highly trained astronauts, for example, are trained in the use of Self-Talk, and it is likely that during the past decade there has not been a single shuttle countdown that did not include the same kinds of words that little Emmaleigh used to solve her problem with math.

A grade-school student going to a class in second-grade math in Scottsdale, Arizona, a Boeing 747 captain piloting his plane toward a safe landing at JFK Airport in New York, and a NASA astronaut en route to the moon, all have something in common: They all use a natural set of self-commands that create focus and self-control. They all use Self-Talk.

Many parents have related stories to me about the

positive effects the simple words of Self-Talk have had in their homes. One couple wrote to tell me about their five-year-old daughter who got up every morning, stood in front of her mirror, and said, "I like myself, I like to be me, I'm happy, and I smile every morning."

Her few words of Self-Talk had produced a wonderful result. Her parents told me that their daughter not only smiled in the morning, she was happy and smiling *most* of the time!

Other parents have told me about the changes they saw in their teenage son or daughter who learned to Self-Talk in a positive way.

One teenage son told his father that he had come home early from being out with his friends when some of the members of the group of young people had been persuaded to take some pills that would "get them high."

When the father asked his son why he had made the decision to come home, his son repeated two of the phrases of Self-Talk that he had learned at home: "I take responsibility for myself. I respect who I am and I know how to say no."

UNLIMITED OPPORTUNITIES FOR SELF-TALK TO HELP

After the publication of my two previous books on the subject of Self-Talk, *What to Say When You Talk to Your Self* and *The Self-Talk Solution,* I was deluged with letters from parents who had used Self-Talk in their homes and taught Self-Talk to their children.

Each time I read one of those letters, I was reminded again of how the Self-Talk that a child learns will crop up almost *anytime*.

Parents found that the Self-Talk their kids were using would *unexpectedly* come to their mind in the middle of a thought at school, during a conversation at home (when in the past an argument would have been the natural response), in sports, during a test, out with friends, getting ready in the morning, on a date, during work time, when they were playing, when a problem came up, talking to a schoolmate, at the dinner table, or at any time a child knew it was time for him to expect the best of himself.

That is a part of the attitude of "self" that the right kind of Self-Talk creates. Once you start using it, Self-Talk comes up *everywhere*. That's the nature of Self-Talk. It becomes a basic part of the intuitive thought process of anyone who practices it.

MAKE SURE *YOUR* SELF-TALK IS THE RIGHT KIND

One mother told me, "My twelve-year-old isn't the problem—*I'm* the problem!" Her *own* past programming had given her so many false or negative beliefs that it was all she could do to overcome them, let alone give positive programs to her own child!

If the mental files in your mind don't always match up with the attitudes that good parenting demands, what can you do?

One thing you can do is to realize that you are working, right now, with the beliefs, attitudes, feelings, and behaviors that *you too* were programmed to have. And most of those programs, if you choose, can be changed or improved. If you want to bring out the best in your kids, make sure you're working with the best of yourself.

Some of the most interesting letters I received from the readers of my previous books were from parents who were using the Self-Talk scripts for "families," "relationships," and "parenting."

They, too, recognized that taking care of their own attitudes about themselves, as parents, would have a lot to do with how well they did.

I had long felt that how well we manage our *own* Self-Talk would play a key role in the success that each of us would achieve in the guidance and upbringing of our kids. Eventually I wrote a script for a Self-Talk cassette entitled "Positive Parenting."

That script of Self-Talk has worked for a lot of parents—and I would like to share it with you.

SOME SPECIAL SELF-TALK, JUST FOR PARENTS

I am an exceptionally good parent! I like being a parent, and it shows in every part of my life.

I accept the responsibilities that parenting brings to my life. I am up to them, I meet them, and I welcome them.

I am good at helping children learn to see themselves in the most positive possible way.

I create harmony and happiness in my home.

I am a good listener. I always listen with interest, understanding, and love. I let children know that I can be talked to—and that I listen!

I am strong and determined, but I am also understanding and supportive.

I never parent with idle threats or forgotten warnings. I can always be counted on to be true to my word.

I understand the difference between punishment, discipline, and training, and I always work to keep them in their proper perspective.

I can be counted on. Because I am reliable and consistent, I greatly increase the assurance of love and security in my home.

I teach values by the examples I set.

I see each day as an opportunity to show, by example, the very best way to live that day.

I never criticize or belittle a child's efforts or ideas.

Instead of expecting perfection, I expect the best that my child has to offer.

I am good at giving rewards, big or small, and at any time at all.

I make it a point to tell each member of my family something special and good about that person each and every day.

I keep my self up, enthusiastic, and in good, healthy spirits.

My own positive attitude about parenting is reflected in everything I do.

I really enjoy being a good parent and experiencing the many joys and benefits that positive parenting brings to my life and to the lives of those I love.

Those few words of Self-Talk have given many parents the lift and encouragement to go one step beyond what they might have done, to be a better parent—that moment or that day! It is through the self-directions that we now give ourselves that we create the attitudes and skills we need to see ourselves and our children in the brightest, most positive way.

AN IMPORTANT TOOL FOR PREDICTIVE PARENTING

Along with using Self-Talk and teaching young people *about* Self-Talk, helping kids put positive Self-Talk into practice is one of the best ways we have ever learned for developing in them positive, lasting attitudes and pictures of capability and self-worth.

When Self-Talk is used along with your words of Predictive Parenting (that *you* say to them), Self-Talk becomes the final weld that seals the best of their programs in their minds. When a child or a young person learns to use positive, productive Self-Talk naturally and unconsciously, that child joins you, the parent, in helping build the strongest possible pictures of value and belief for himself.

In time, a young person's Self-Talk becomes a natural part of how he thinks. It becomes a new habit of identifying himself with his most promising potential.

The use of positive, healthy, self-*directing* Self-Talk is one of the most worthwhile habits we could ever help our children learn.

And *that* is the goal of teaching Self-Talk to the children in our lives. Taking the time to help our children see themselves in the most positive and worthwhile way is Predictive Parenting at its best.

Chapter 20

Predictive Parenting in Your Home

When parents decide to use Predictive Parenting in their homes, they usually find a wealth of ways to put it to work.

Here are some of the best ways parents have found to practice Predictive Parenting:

1. Use Words and Pictures That Help Children Build the Best Pictures of Themselves in Their Minds.

Many parents have found that they really enjoy getting into the habit of talking to their kids in a way that helps them build files of the best pictures of themselves in their minds.

When you talk to your kids, paint pictures in their minds. Show them the best of themselves and repaint the picture over and over. Never let up. The pictures that you share with them are some of the most important pictures that they will ever learn to create for themselves. Let them see themselves in the most promising, exciting, positive way possible.

Show them their best. Show them their strengths. Show them their courage, their endurance, their abilities and capabilities. Show them their value—show them their worth. Show them their true selves.

Remember, too, to look for *their* input. They are painting the picture too. As they grow, have new experiences, learn more, and see themselves in different ways, much of what they are adding will help you know how to help *them* fill the picture in.

Every chance you have, repaint the picture. Help them fill their files with the most precise pictures of self-belief you can possibly give them.

Help them picture themselves overcoming their fears. Show them pictures of themselves as being exceptional, extraordinary, unique, special, outstanding, productive, valuable, healthy, and important.

Tell them stories of what they can become. Whether they are three, twelve, or seventeen, start painting the picture and let them see it again and again.

2. Talk About the Subject of "How to Make Things Work Better."

After using Predictive Parenting techniques in their home and putting them into practice for several months, one couple told me that both of them and their two children now look forward to their family discussions as some of the best times they spend together.

"We used to take some time each week to discuss activities, school, problems, and responsibilities around the house," the mother said. "But we've started to look at a lot of those things differently now. Our two kids (ages seven and nine) have already started to figure out that they're a part of making things work for all of us."

Few parenting tools work better than the family discussion—if that discussion is aimed in the right direction.

Families that practice Predictive Parenting as a basic part of family life have clear-cut directions to follow. We have learned that children need—and *want*—structure in their lives. When parents are consistent and positive, with a purpose in mind that every member of the family is aware of, they automatically create more structure. And that in turn leads to more security and "safety" in the children's minds.

It is that same sense of "organized direction" that Predictive Parenting develops that lowers temperatures and reduces some of the problems of high-volume chaos in their homes. One couple told me that the noise level of their family talks has dropped by half.

In some families, that in itself is a major step forward. A father who was attending one of my seminars told the group, during a discussion period, that he was sure that if he would let them, his kids would use microphones, an amplifier, and loudspeakers when they were talking at the dinner table.

I hope that father found the solution he was looking for by applying some "predictive" ideas in his household. He also told our seminar group that the first thing he was going to do when he got home that night was to stop saying ever again something he had said to his kids for years, "You don't know how to talk without shouting at each other!"

3. Use Predictive Parenting As a New Way to Deal with Daily Problems.

Much of the Predictive Parenting that parents practice deals with the "positive"—building self-esteem, listening better, talking to children with more encouraging words, and so on. But much of it also deals with handling the day-to-day problems that are part and parcel of any home.

When a child runs in the door with a skinned knee or

a bruised ego, what will you say? When a youngster can't get his homework done on time, what will you tell him? What we say to our kids when they have a problem will either ignore the problem, make it worse, or help solve it.

Even when we are not aware of it, what we say at the time will also put another message into the child's mental filing cabinet that will tell him or her how to expect us to deal with the same kind of problem next time around.

Vicky, a sixteen-year-old girl who had fallen in with the wrong friends, was skipping school, staying out without permission, and starting to get into trouble. Her parents brought her to a talk I was giving in hopes that the three of them could stop the problem before it got worse.

During a break Vicky told me she couldn't understand why her parents wouldn't listen to her before. "Finally, after all this time, they want to help," she told me, "but I've always had to deal with my problems by myself. I don't think they've ever been all that interested in *anything* I've done."

It's no wonder Vicky's parents were having difficulties dealing with Vicky's problems. Their past messages to her had convinced Vicky long ago that her parents didn't care.

I remember the time when two of my friends were shocked when their own daughter, an eighteen-year-old in her last year of high school moved out of their home and in with friends. Her reason? "You don't talk to me anyway, why should I stay here?"

And I will never forget the young father who told me of the sudden breakthrough of awareness he felt when his little four-year-old son brought a broken toy to him and said, *"You won't help me fix this, will you?"* That four-year-old had already learned to believe that his father was the wrong person to go to with a problem.

One of the best ways of making sure you will be able to help with the *big* problems that come is to let your kids know that you are there to help them with the *little* problems. They may seem small and unimportant at the time, but the way you deal with them will predict to your child how you will help them with the rest of their problems.

BIG PROBLEMS FROM LITTLE PROBLEMS GROW

There is another reason why parents will start using Predictive Parenting words and ideas for dealing with the small problems their children encounter. They find that by treating the little problems in a more "interested" way, they are often able to stop a small problem from becoming a big problem—before it ever has a chance to grow.

The next time your child comes to you with a problem, stop for just a moment and ask yourself, "If what I do next will affect my child down the road, how should I handle this problem *today*?"

4. Give Your Children a Better Way to Get Along with Each Other.

Harmony in the home is a luxury for some parents that they no longer expect to achieve. I have often heard a parent say, "What I wouldn't do for some peace and quiet now and then!" Unless we begin to work at changing what is causing the disharmony in the first place, peace and quiet *now and then* is the best we can hope for.

When we talk about getting children to be cooperative, we have to be realistic, of course. Kids are kids, and part of the process of growing up includes arguments; hurt feelings; self-centered notions; insensitive words said to someone else; a sometimes total lack of consideration for another kid's possessions, time, or feelings; and all of the other upheavals and outbreaks that sibling rivalries and just plain "being kids" creates.

The reason for much of this uproar is that children and young people are constantly growing and changing. Their bodies, their moods, their needs, their identities, their expectations of others and what is expected of *them*—all of these are changing.

Packed into such a few short years, that much change would make *anyone* hard to handle now and then. If you or I as adults had to endure as much change in two or three years as a child faces, without letup, for eighteen or more years, *we* would probably be less manageable than our children!

So our objective as Predictive Parents is not to suddenly create blissful demeanors of quiet contentment on our children's smiling faces. It is to give our children a way of dealing with some of their frustrations in a calmer, more productive way.

Even a minor change in a child's attitude can bring welcome relief. A positive, upward shift in a child's self-esteem can create the beginnings of a different, more settled mood for that child.

But when we begin practicing Predictive Parenting, it is the changes in how *we* act toward our kids that creates the first noticeable difference.

One mother told me, somewhat embarrassed, how one day she caught herself teaching her five-year-old daughter exactly the wrong kind of behavior. The mother stopped herself short when she was saying to her daughter, "How many times have I told you not to shout or hit your sister?!," while at the same time the mother was shouting the words and hitting her daughter on the arm to drive her point home.

TEN WAYS TO BUILD HARMONY IN THE HOME

In spite of the fact that Predictive Parenting is an *attitude* of parenting and not a set of rules or techniques, there are many ideas that Predictive Parents can use to help their children get along better.

Here are ten good ideas for developing smoother relationships in your home:

1. *Keep your voice down.*

2. *Give each person a turn to talk at the table.*

3. *If you get angry and are getting ready to make a parenting mistake, go to your room.*

4. *Always treat every family member with equal respect.*

5. *Set rules about rooms, privacy, possessions, and individual rights and stick by them.*

6. *Practice and use the Rule of Personal Responsibility in every possible opportunity.*

7. *Never argue about an argument. Arbitrate and diffuse it.*

8. *Always act the way you want your children to act.*

9. *Be consistent and be ready to explain when you can't be.*

10. *Instead of focusing on the negative results of not getting along, show the benefits of doing it right.*

To a conscious, aware, positive Predictive Parent, every suggestion on that list has behind it a wealth of understanding of the programming processes of the human mind.

It is not the calm quiet voice you use when you speak that does the job all by itself—*it is the unconscious reassurance to the child's subconscious mind that you are in control.*

It is not the "rules" you set about your children's right to privacy and possessions—*it is the recognition of those rights that you create in your child's mind.*

It is not only giving each child or adult his or her "turn to speak" that ultimately creates the harmony—*it is each person's awareness that he or she, too, is important and that when they talk, others will listen to them.*

One of the many benefits of the objective of creating lasting changes in the harmony of your home life is that once you start working at it, any effort you put into it usually takes less time than fighting the problems in the first place.

Another one of those benefits, if you work at it, is that somewhere down the line you do get more of that "peace and quiet" you were looking for.

5. Give Yourself a Better Way to Teach the Tools of Living.

Learning Predictive Parenting clearly has its value. And understanding the concept of Predictive Parenting is advisable for any parent.

But what about giving our kids the day-to-day practical everyday tools they need to help them through their daily lives—the tools that go beyond theory and work for them now?

An important role of "parenting" is the role of teaching those tools. And it is in this role that Predictive Parenting gives us some of our most immediate rewards. There is no child who learns better than the child whose personal potential is understood and cared for.

Predictive Parents recognize that it is essential that we give our children strong positive images of themselves in the files of their minds. But we also recognize that we have to give our children and young people the practical knowledge it takes to get them where they are going.

That's why a Predictive father or mother will say, "Let me help you understand that," instead of saying, "Ask someone else, I'm busy." Or a Predictive Parent will say, "I'll show you how it works, and then you can explain it back to me."

Here is a partial list of things that would help any child—when he or she understood them—have a better preparation for adulthood. As you read through this list, see if you can find the *one* similarity that each of these individual "tools of living" have in common.

An understanding of

> Schoolwork
> Friendships
> The role of sports in our lives
> The reason to dress in a certain way
> How to deal with problems
> History
> What to pack in a lunchbox
> What you see on television
> The effective use of language and how to
>   communicate
> Why there are laws and why they should be
>   followed
> How to put together a jigsaw puzzle
> The importance of tradition
> The value of money
> Why someone is a friend one day and not the next
> Spiritual beliefs
> Why a bedroom should be organized
> Why it's wrong to tell a lie

Who makes the rules and why
What makes marriages work and what makes
    them fail
Why some people are poor and other people have
    more than they need
Mathematics
The importance of good health
Creativity
Why there is a speed limit
Why Thomas Edison was important
Why they can't stay up late on a school night

That list could go on indefinitely. It is a list of a few examples of commonplace subjects and questions that give us the opportunity to bring out important parts of our children's potential knowledge.

All of the examples on that list are areas *that affect their understanding of life—that are potentially influenced by parental opinion.*

How many of the "tools of living" would you like your child to learn by the *chance opinions* of someone else?

The tools of living are the knowledge and experience we have collected from our past and gleaned from the world around us today.

Why *was* Thomas Edison important? Was it because he invented the light bulb? What are friendships for? What would we like our kids to know about the value of money? Why *is* it "wrong" to tell a lie? What *does* make marriage work? Why should we value our health? Why *are* there laws? And why *can't* they stay up late on a school night?

Our kids need our input—our opinions—and our ideas. We don't have to be scholars and we don't need "superminds" to give our children the tools and guidance that they need from us.

We only have to recognize that we have a right and an obligation to make sure each of our children has the right tools to live by.

Those parents who have decided to take an active role in the conscious development of their children's potential learn to take advantage of every opportunity that comes to them to get their messages across.

Every detail we help our children understand is another tool they can use. They will learn a lot from other sources, of course, but what about those tools that need the influence of a strong, caring parenting mind?

For the child, the tools of living will never be in better hands than yours. Those tools give you the opportunity to exercise your options as a Predictive Parent.

They give you the chance to teach each of the tools of life to your children in their most positive, meaningful, and worthwhile ways—in line with the goals that *you* set.

That doesn't mean you spend your valuable parenting time trying to override the knowledge that your children receive at school and from their other sources of learning. It means that you make the decision to play a part in adding your sense of positive, *predictive* direction to the rest of the knowledge that they receive.

6. Give Your Children the Words That Help Predict Their Most Positive Futures.

Many years ago, when my son Gregory was six or seven years old, he and I began to play a game each day while I shaved in the morning. I wanted to find a way to teach little Greg what some of the words meant that our family might use around the home.

These were words that identified concepts that I felt were important to teach kids, and I wanted to make those concepts easy to understand—and fun to learn.

So I developed the idea of a friendly animal character that I called "Eloquent the Elephant." It was Eloquent's particular distinction that she had a trunkful of words, and each morning Eloquent would give Greg and me another of those new words to chew on. Each morning

Greg would come into my dressing room with his little stack of index cards and a pencil and ask what today's new word was.

And each day Eloquent dipped into her trunkful of words and came up with a beauty. They were words like *positive, sharing, self-belief, enthusiasm, vision, care, motivation,* and *unlimited.* Most of the words had values that I had attached to them of course (undoubtedly some of the same values that *my* parents had attached to them before me).

I would give Greg the word of the day, and he would carefully print it out on one of his index cards. Then he and I would discuss that word, its definition, how it was used, and what that word really *meant* in our everyday lives. He would then pull out the card with the word that he had learned the day before and tell me what he remembered about it.

I have often thought about how much that simple time together each morning came to mean in Greg's life as he grew older. Many times in the years since I have heard Greg talking about one subject or another and heard those same words crop up time and time again—not just as descriptions of what he was talking about but as essential parts of his life that he had come to appreciate and understand.

There were many occasions in his young life when he dealt with problems and situations in a surprisingly successful way—and I have often been thankful for Eloquent the Elephant and her trunkful of words.

Now when I discuss with parents the importance of getting their messages across on such subjects as the building of character in a young person's mind, I am reminded of many of the same words my young son and I discussed way back then.

Some of the most obvious attributes of "character," for example, are *honesty, caring, consideration, manners, self-esteem, giving, receiving, listening, understanding, initiative, accomplishment, and compassion.* If you have those words, and what they mean, in the structure of your life, and if you live those words each day, you increase your chances of living an exceptional life.

These are just a few of the kinds of words that Predictive Parents give to their children so that they, too, can tuck them into *their* files:

Honesty gives us a faithful picture of who we are and the world we live in.

Caring lets us know the importance of others.

Consideration helps us take the time to recognize what others are dealing with in their lives.

Manners helps us act in the most fitting and appropriate way in any situation.

Self-esteem shows us our greatest value and helps us recognize the value in others.

Giving helps us share some of how we are and what we are with others.

Receiving allows us to accept the sharing that others, too, need in their lives.

Listening makes us aware of the thoughts and the feelings of others and gives us a way to learn about life and about ourselves.

Understanding gives us insight. It helps us look inside and see what is really there.

Initiative is the gift we give to ourselves that gets us started and keeps us moving. It is the spark that ignites our objectives and fans them into our achievements.

Accomplishment is the way we measure the value of the time we spend doing anything we do.

Compassion gives us the human quality by which we learn to accept others.

It will be up to you to place on these and similar words the values and meanings that are important to you. But if you leave the teaching of the value and meaning of concepts up to someone else, it is likely that your son or daughter will adopt someone *else's* point of view or never get the message at all! It would be a shame for any young person to have to grow up without some of life's most basic building blocks being firmly set in place.

If your children "own" those words, and many more like them, and make them a part of the permanent files in their minds, they will have an understanding that will improve and enhance the rest of the learning in their lives.

AN INVESTMENT OF *YOUR* TIME IN *THEIR* FUTURES

Of all the comments I hear from parents who have put Predictive Parenting ideas to work in their homes, the most frequent is, "It is always more than worth the effort." Predictive Parenting works; it makes a difference!

If your own efforts at parenting in a more predictive way were to do nothing more than make a minor change tomorrow in how you saw your role as a parent and in how you dealt with your child as a result, then your child's future would be better for it.

Predictive Parenting is not some simple list of rules to follow. There are good ideas you can begin using today or tomorrow in your own home—but Predictive Parenting offers no simple mechanical solution to achieving a successful family life. Nevertheless, if you want to take a strong stand in the development or direction of your child's life—if you want to practice Predictive Parenting in your own life with your children—you can.

More than anything else the success of Predictive Parenting in your home will be the result of your decision to be aware of it, take a stand—and act on it.

There is every good reason for you to exercise the right you have; to play the most important role you can possibly play in the development of your child's greatest potential. I have yet to find a single reason not to do it.

Chapter 21

Great Moments of Opportunity

Once you have become aware of *how* Predictive Parenting works, the next step is to make the decision to look for opportunities to practice being a Predictive Parent. When you start looking, you'll find that the opportunities aren't hard to find.

I mentioned earlier that spending half an hour a day in the company of our children gives us more than *ten thousand* minutes of direct parenting time in just one year.

That's a lot of moments of opportunity. What we do with each of them will ultimately determine how well we do at the job of parenting—and how well our children do because of it.

But we have also learned that Predictive Parenting is more an attitude *about* parenting than it is a set of how-to's or step-by-step techniques. There are ideas and techniques that help, of course, many of which we have discussed here. But it is our *awareness,* our *attitude,* and our *decisions* about our parenting that will help us find the opportunities and do something with them.

One of the most important attributes of Predictive Parenting is that it offers each of us a way to asses and choose our own individual parenting methods and goals—without it trying to tell us how we should raise our kids. Predictive Parenting says, "Do it *your* way—but be aware of how the mind of a child works and how you affect and influence that mind."

That's one of the things that parents appreciate about Predictive Parenting. It puts the choices, the rights, and the responsibility of parenting *right where they belong*—with *each* of us.

So it is your choice to find and make the best of those great moments of opportunity—or not. The following suggestions will help:

1. Look for Opportunities to Practice Predictive Parenting Whenever You Talk to Your Children or Deal with Them in Any Way.

The list of possible opportunities to deal predictively with your children would fill a book by itself. How many times in a single day or a week or a month do you, in some way, affect, talk to, or influence your children?

I asked one couple how often they were consciously aware of what they were learning to say to their kids. The mother's answer was, "How many minutes are there in a day?"

The opportunities are endless. Once we become aware of them, once we learn to see the smallest details of our children's lives as opportunities to affect and predict positively their futures—those opportunities begin to present themselves to us at every moment of our parenting day.

The toughest problem or the most minor circumstance gives us another chance to give them another advantage.

If I were asked to make a list of those times or circumstances when we could *not* create a benefit by practicing Predictive Parenting with our kids, it would take no time at all to write the list. There would be nothing on it.

2. Identify the Specific Problem Areas That You Would Like to Give Yourself Some Help On.

The items you put on this list should fall clearly into the "problem" category—any tough problem that you or your kids have been having major trouble with.

These would typically include such things as severe behavior problems—the kind that are seriously affecting a child's or young person's school or personal life, an attitude problem that is clearly getting worse instead of better, a consistent problem of communication between your child and you or your child and his other parent, a problem that has arisen because of a separation or a divorce, and so on.

Lesser difficulties that are the result of average day-to-day situations are not really "problems" (although we call them that, and they certainly seem like it at the time). They are, when we view them from a more positive perspective, just normal situations of life that we run into when we raise a family.

3. Look at Each of the Problem Areas You Have Put on Your List and Decide What You Are Going to Do Next—Predictively—to Deal with Each of Them.

4. Make a Second List of Specific "Areas of Positive Growth" That You Want to Work on with Each of Your Children.

This list would include items such as "Give more positive reinforcement to Bobby about his math," "Talk to Susan and encourage her about her hopes for finding a part-time job," "Help Rick with his attitude about his looks," "Schedule a family 'activities' discussion and put some positive life into it."

5. Make a Specific Decision About What You Are Going to Do in Each Area You Have Listed and

Write Down Your Solution or the Action You Are Going to Take.

Think about it, decide what you are going to do, write it down, and do it. The first step is deciding what we want to do. But no one should have to remind us that actually doing the things we write on the list is the part of the job that gets the results.

6. Ask Your Kids What Areas *They* Would Like to Work On—with Your Support—and Discuss the Problem or the Objective with Them.

The more you help your kids understand what you are doing—and why—the better this works. If they are old enough, and if you can help them understand what you are doing as a Predictive Parent, they will also figure out that *they* will benefit.

7. Show Your Children How Their Own Self-Talk Can Help Them Each Day and Encourage Them to See Themselves in the Very Best Way.

8. Enlist the Cooperation and Support of Your Spouse or Mate.

This is more than a suggestion of a way that you can put Predictive Parenting into practice; sharing a common understanding of Predictive Parenting with your spouse or mate is essential.

When I conduct a seminar on Predictive Parenting, among the kinds of members who make up the audience are single parents who have come alone or with a friend, married parents who attend together, and one or the other member of a married couple who is attending the seminar by herself or by himself.

Without exception, a parent who is married and who attends the seminar alone will ask me what she or he can do to get her or his husband or wife (who didn't attend the seminar) interested in Predictive Parenting. I often hear the comment, "I'm really interested in doing some things that will help our kids. But I just can't get my husband (or wife) to go along with it."

When that happens, the best ideas of parenting often fall short of the mark because *both* of the parents aren't operating with the same goals—or the same interest.

The problem is understandable. Some parents have gotten so used to hearing about *this* new idea or *that* new technique for some form or another of "personal improvement" that they become wary. Even the most loving husband or wife can say, "Not *another* self-improvement seminar" or "You think we ought to try *what*?!"

The result is that one of the parents thinks something is a great idea and the other parent is sure it won't work—and unconsciously sets out to prove that it *doesn't*.

Predictive Parenting is not a "success system." *It is simply a better understanding of how and why kids and parents do what they do*—and the results of our words and actions—which we are only recently becoming generally aware of.

Or there are other circumstances, when one parent is simply more interested in working at learning to do a better job of parenting than the other parent is. I have heard good, conscientious parents say, "I'm doing the best I can and that's all I'm going to do." Or "The way I was raised was good enough for my parents. The way I'm raising my kids is good enough for me."

That *is* their right, of course. And when someone tells me something like that, the best I can do is tell him or her what we have learned about kids and the brain and programming and influence and children's futures. But if he does not choose to listen, that is his right as a parent.

You may choose to see it differently, of course. If you are trying to get the cooperation of someone in your life to work with you in creating a better style of parenting then it is also your right to do everything you can to win that cooperation.

Both parents working together to achieve the same end will always create more successful results than one parent trying to do it alone.

Fortunately, the basic concept of how parents program and predict their children's futures by what they say and do isn't a difficult concept to explain. It makes sense, it is logical, it is psychologically, physiologically, and neurologically sound, and it doesn't conflict with even the most fundamental religious beliefs. (The same concept, without the technological reasons why it worked, was expressed in the Bible several thousand years ago.)

Always remember, however, that each of us is the product of our own previous programming and conditioning. I have met many parents whose own prior programming was so strong that it simply would not *allow* any *new* ideas or programs to have their say.

What is most important is that you do everything you can to enlist the support of your spouse or mate in everything that affects the raising and the influencing of your children.

The result of the parenting influences—the programs that *each* of you will give to your children—will play a role of such importance in your children's futures that we can only guess at the consequences of *not* working together to achieve the best possible result!

And the potential, positive results of working together as a strong, unified, Predictive force in your children's lives is so worthwhile that it makes any effort you have to make to work at parenting together worth every moment of effort you commit.

9. Learn to See Each Day As an Important Day in Your Child's Life.

You can only make every day count if you know how important every day is. I have all too often heard a parent say, *after* it was too late, "If only I had done things differently." Or, "If only I had the chance to do it over again."

That feeling is not unusual. Most parents wish, at one time or another, that they could have done a few things—or a *lot* of things—differently.

If we really understand the value of the time we are able to spend with our children, and how amazingly fleeting that time can be, we will live with the awareness to make every day and every moment count.

Chapter 22

Your Personal Parenting Prediction

What will you, in your own way, predict for the future of your child or children? What will you put into the files in that vast mental filing room in their subconscious minds?

WHAT WILL YOU PREDICT?

There are three ways that our skills of Predictive Parenting can help us. One is the way in which we help our children see themselves now in a more positive way. The second is in how we help forestall—or prevent—future problems, long before they come up. And the third is in the expression of potential that we help our kids find and develop within themselves.

It is these three benefits that we offer our children and young people when we practice parenting in a way that suggests to them—in everything we say and do:

1. *Who they really are*

2. *The choices they will make each and every day*

3. *The potential they have in front of them*

If you had to write your own list of predictions for your child, what would you write on that list?

What would your predictions say about how well your child will do in school, the kinds of relationships he will attract, how well you and that child will communicate and get along with each other, what successes he will create in the life ahead of him, what his beliefs will be about his abilities and skills yet to come, and what his level of self-worth, self-esteem, and self-belief will be?

Your child's future will be the result of the choices he makes. And there will be an endless number of choices to make.

Every choice—big or small—that your child ever makes will be the result of what he finds when he measures them against the files that are stored in the filing cabinets of his subconscious mind.

Our words to our children become *pathways in the mind.* Whatever is stored in those files will determine the choices, the beliefs, the attitudes, the feelings, the actions, the directions, and the everyday success—or lack of it—of your child.

That is how the brain operates. Even if we were to ignore it, the brain would continue to operate in the same exact way day after day. It has no choice. Whatever *we* put into those files of the mind will influence and direct every facet of that child's or young person's life.

THE DIFFERENCE THAT YOU MAKE

You as a parent can, if you choose, make a difference in your child that will surpass any other influence in his or her young life. (If you are a teacher, I would suggest that your influence will be exceptionally important, second only to the parents themselves.)

The difference you make in your child's life today and tomorrow gives you a responsibility of untold magnitude and importance.

You are not just raising children to "get through life." You are raising people who will one day have a vote in the future of their own lives—and, in all possibility, in the future of this planet for generations to come.

THE THRESHOLD OF A NEW AWARENESS

As we raise our children in a more positive and Predictive way, we are doing more than raising the children themselves. Along with our goals and expectations for our children we are also raising our expectations for our children's education, from what is said to them and what they are taught in day care centers to what is said and taught to them in schools—and beyond.

We are already beginning to see the effects of Predictive Parenting and Predictive Teaching—in homes and in schools.

The mother of a six-year-old first-grader told me that her young son's teacher called her to discuss something her son had said to her in class. The boy's parents had taught him the value of Self-Talk and positive self-direction.

One day in school, after the teacher had told a young girl that she "would never get it right," the young boy said to the teacher, "If you tell her that, she never will."

I suspect that before long, more parents and more

teachers will understand the value of their Predictive words.

Teachers will begin to teach their pupils about self-esteem and self-belief, with a stronger sense of purpose and direction when they teach those concepts. In time, they will learn to use more of the words that create those attitudes and beliefs in children's minds.

Parents will begin to teach their children the same kinds of "self-directions" at home—and in time it will be more natural to teach a child *self-worth* than it will be to prove to a child, unwittingly, that he is somehow less than he could or should be.

Eventually more of us will come to understand that if there is a new "awareness" that is going to do anything to help us solve the problems we face, the answers will come from the children we are preparing today.

In the past we have done our best to get along as well as we could with what we had to work with. Some of what we had to work with did not do a great deal to help us.

Most of us, if we are honest about it, have lived with mental filing cabinets that are filled with files, many of which, if we were given the choice today, would never have been put there at all.

There is no reason to pass any of those same kinds of files on to our young. They don't need them. They will have enough obstacles to deal with without them.

Without the files of doubt, indifference, and negative influence—and the acceptance of limited potential—there is no telling what a generation or two could do.

WHAT IS THE "FUTURE" THAT YOU COULD PREDICT?

What you say, what you *predict* by what you say and what you do, will make a difference. Your "personal parenting prediction" will count—in almost unimaginable ways—in the days ahead and in the future of your child.

What you do and say next, and for every parenting day you have thereafter, will be important.

A number of our most respected scientists and philosophers have told us that we only learn to use 10 or 15 percent of the capabilities of our minds.

If enough of us recognize that we have, in the past, been training our children to operate at something less than only a minor percentage of their potential, just imagine what could happen if we gave them the chance to operate at something closer to their best.

Even given the right tools of unlimited self-belief and positive life-changing self-direction to work with, I doubt that any of us would expect our children to change the world overnight. But I would like to be around to see what they do.

I was asked one time by a friend of mine what I would say to parents if I were to write a book about parenting. What would I write to parents, as my one, most important message? My answer was as simple as the message itself, and it is my message to you: Of all the influences that predict your child's future, the most important influence is you.

YOU make the difference.

For more information on "Predictive Parenting" or
"Predictive Teaching" Seminar programs, or to contact
Dr. Shad Helmstetter, write to:

The Self-Talk Institute
P.O. Box 5165
Scottsdale, AZ 85261